# COLOUR
# power

# COLOUR
# power

Top tips for enhancing every area
of your life through colour

PHILIPPA MERIVALE

*This book is dedicated*
*to Jamie, with love.*

UK ISBN 1-84333-699-5

US ISBN 1-84333-715-0

Project Editor Alison Moss
Design by Isobel Gillan
Production by Susan Sutterby

Printed and bound in Hong Kong

# contents

# introduction

COLOUR HAS BEEN USED since the earliest days of our history as a curative, able to heal the mind as well as the body. We are all aware of the recuperative effect of sunlight in healing wounds and uplifting the spirits, and its role in the body's manufacture of Vitamin D. The different wavelengths of light, which we perceive as colours, affect every aspect of our physiology. Some colours arouse our energy while others encourage us to sleep. Colour also helps us to interpret our world. On a geographical level the natural colours of a landscape and the social colours of its people distinguish one country and culture from another. On a seasonal level the high colours of summer feed and energize us, and their winter absence shuts us down.

Not only our eyes but all the cells of our bodies are sensitive to colour. Our circulation, nervous and digestive systems and all the vital organs are constantly influenced and altered by the effects of the colours that we wear, eat, drink and see in the world around us. Colours influence the way we think and feel; even more significantly, the colours that attract us the most reveal much about our inner selves. Colour can be learned and understood as a language that reveals truths, which are the same regardless of creed, country or race.

How often have you heard of someone showing their *true colours*, feeling *green with envy*, having a touch of the *blues* or being *tickled pink*? You may *see red* if you are angry, or feel *off colour* when your energy is low. A vibrant, energetic personality is described as *colourful*; your political affiliations may be *red*, *green* or *blue*.

These tags that we give spontaneously to our own and others' behaviour and feelings recur in different languages worldwide and hint at the real meaning colour has for us. Colour symbolism remains constant, with very few differences, throughout cultures that otherwise appear to have little in common. It is a universal currency, which variously reflects our feelings, our thoughts, our memories.

A brief analysis of our colour preferences provides us with penetrating insights into our current state of heart, mind and soul. Our *true colours* are the fast route to self-knowledge; they open a direct line to the resolution of many of the difficulties in our lives. While techniques of healing through colour have been used with great success, in times ancient and modern, all around the world, it is their ability as a tool to help with day-to-day pressures and to improve the quality of life that has perhaps the widest and the most universal application. Anyone can learn the language of colour: it is really very simple.

The pages of this book will prompt you to look at the colours that draw you in a way that you might not have seen them before. They may encourage you to liven up your diet or your walls; but they will also do more. Once understood, colour can paint a map of the psyche, a force comprising more than our casual use of the word 'psychology' implies: the Greek source of this word means the breath, the life, the soul.

When you let its power into your life, colour will improve your confidence and your health, harmonize your relationships and bring greater satisfaction, love, compassion and abundance into life at work and at home. I hope this book will alert you to the potent support of colour, so that it will enrich your life – as it has mine and countless others.

# colour affects your body

COLOUR IS THE EXPRESSION of the vital, generative, life-force of light that sustains us. What we perceive as a particular colour is actually a wavelength of active, moving energy. We can see about 40 per cent of the colours in the full spectrum of sunlight. While the colours outside that range, such as ultra-violet and infra-red, are potentially harmful, those inside it have specific and beneficial effects on our physiology. Each wavelength has its unique signature and character, which impacts on us in a specific way.

The cells most receptive to light are those contained in the eyes, most particularly the photoreceptors of the retina, nerve cells that respond to light in a way that can be compared to the coating on the surface of a camera film. These are the cones, each of which respond to one of three colours of light – red, green or blue – by bleaching and dissolving when the light reaches them. This sends a stimulus to the visual cortex at the back of the brain, and the infinite combinations of red, green and blue messages triggered by the differing cones enable us to perceive an incredible range of varied hues.

While about 80 per cent of this stimulus travels to the visual cortex at the back of the skull for the purposes of sight, the remainder stimulates the hypothalamus, the pituitary and pineal glands and the limbic system in the brain. Through these channels, messages travel to different regions of the body, influencing our hormonal activity and our emotions according to the colour which is their source.

While we receive the greater part of the colour energy we need through our eyes, the skin also absorbs light rays. So, too, do our inner cells and consequently colour can reach us through the foods we eat. Each colour will have a different effect on the cells. Red and orange rays, for instance, with their long and powerful wavelengths, have a stimulating effect, which can result in increased appetite, a raising of the blood pressure, improvement in circulation, and greater body warmth. At the other end of the spectrum

of light, blue and violet, with their short, unobtrusive waveforms, have a calming and cooling effect. They soothe agitated cells and feelings, relieve soreness, reduce the blood pressure and slow us down.

The colours around us are in constant interaction with our bodies as well as our feelings and thoughts. Familiarity with their qualities will enable you to increase your intake of whichever colours you need. You will soon come to recognize the colours that resonate most comfortably with you, and what these colours have to show you. Each colour also has another colour, which is its opposite and complementary. If you look for a while at the colour yellow, for example, and then close your eyes, you will see an after-image of its complementary colour violet, which has a natural balancing effect on the first colour. Technically, each pair of complementary colours contain a balance of all the three primary rays whose combinations comprise the full spectrum. In any context where you bring colour consciously into your life, it is helpful to understand the balancing of these complementary pairs. Used together, in your diet, your clothing, your surroundings or as a remedial agent, these can restore the balance of your body.

## colour affects your moods and explains who you are

THE COLOURS YOU CHOOSE can guide you towards a better understanding of yourself and your friends, because they are an intimate part of your being. A Handel aria and a track by the Rolling Stones are characterized by very different sets of waveforms, and we would have little doubt about the differing effects of these waveforms on our mood and on our relative state of activity or calm. We would also be aware that a person's preference for one or the other of these choices of sound would tell us something about his character. Like music, each of us has our predominant chord, or quality; and this can be recognized and understood through the colours we love.

Colour, like sound, is an energy that lives and moves. The colours around you, in your clothes, the walls of your rooms, your garden or the light in the sky, beam waveforms of certain shapes and frequencies, which are absorbed into your body. These affect not just your bodily activities but also the way you feel.

So, from the outside inward, colour brings its energy towards you, variously lifting your spirits, encouraging you towards enthusiasm, sharpening your thoughts, lulling you to sleep. Colour also works from the inside outward: light resonates with each person individually. While everyone has colours that attract them from time to time, altering with mood, changes of health or fashion, there is also a deeper level of interaction. Each individual recognizes certain rays that continue to feel comfortable and familiar through time. Whatever your race, skin colour or creed, your truly favourite colours uncover the real you, your gifts and strengths, fears and hopes. This is because the universe is a field of energy in which everything has its individual note. When a colour consistently attracts you, its waveform is in resonance with yours. You feel in tune with its quality, because that quality is also part of who you are and how you express yourself. Through the aura (see opposite), we receive the energy wavelengths we need and also, unconsciously, project the colours that speak for us. The energy of light, the source of all colour, thus has the capacity to penetrate your consciousness, or your spirit, like a gentle laser beam and to throw light on the parts of yourself that your conscious mind has often failed to see.

You will notice, as you leaf through these pages, that you are generally drawn to some colours above others: you may be predominantly a blue person rather than a red one; a violet one rather than a gold. This is because your personal quality is a vibration, a vibe, whose colours clarify your individual needs and enable you to appreciate your authentic self, allowing you to act consciously and purposefully instead of just reacting to circumstances.

# the chakras and the aura

THE OTHER, MORE subtle, channel through which light interacts with us is the system of chakras and the aura, which together comprise the subtle energy mechanism of the body. From the crown of your head, down your spine to the coccyx at the base, there is a series of energy wheels spinning around. These are called 'chakras', or 'energy centres' or 'energy stations', because they are located at the points where lines of universal light-energy meet and are drawn into the body. This vital force then travels through meridians, or energy channels, to different areas of the body.

Each chakra corresponds to a particular location on the body and also to one of the seven traditional colours of the rainbow, each drawing in energy of a specific ray, or colour. In perfect health, there would be an uninterrupted movement of energy flowing through all the centres – a perfect rainbow. In practice, all of us have certain areas where, for many different reasons, the energy becomes blocked. The aim of colour therapy is to revitalize the entire system by encouraging the free flowing of energy at each chakra.

- The root chakra, located at the base of the spine, corresponds with the colour red. This is our connection with earth and the primary centre of our physical energy. The colour complementary to red is green.

- The sacral chakra, located in the lower part of the gut, corresponds with orange. This area influences the colon and the digestive system. The colour complementary to orange is blue.

- The solar plexus chakra is situated just above the navel: this centre relates to yellow. This station is associated with the functions of mental as well as physical assimilation, and with the nervous system. The colour complementary to yellow is violet.

- The heart chakra is associated with the colour green. This is the centre of emotion and feeling, and of integration between the earthbound stations and the higher centres of awareness, where personality meets soul. The colour complementary to green is red or pink; and many people have associated pink with the heart.

- The throat chakra is nourished by a pale sapphire blue. This area is the meeting point between the mind and the heart, and it relates to communication and speech. The colour complementary to blue is orange or peach.

- The brow chakra, located around the forehead, corresponds to the colour indigo. This centre has to do with the finer senses and with the empowered communication that comes when we find inner authority. It also relates to deep seeing and the link with other realms. The colour complementary to indigo is a mixture between yellow and orange, which could be described as gold or amber.

- The crown chakra, at the top of the head, relates to the colour violet. It is concerned with the mind, the thinking; and also with the integration and wholeness that follows when the individual finds a balance between physical and spiritual concerns. The colour complementary to violet is yellow.

The aura, which like the physical body is fed by the chakras, is an emanation of energy radiating into the atmosphere around you. This is the reason why colour crops up so readily in language: colours relate to physical, emotional and mental states, which are reflected in the quality of energy we radiate around us. If we describe a person as *yellow bellied*, it is because the fear he feels surrounds him as a cloud of yellow. The chakras feed the aura as the currents feed the ocean. This is a living, moving energy system in constant movement. When movement stops, this is where blockages begin. If these imbalances are not redressed, the blockages will eventually manifest as physical symptoms. For any physical cure to have a lasting effect, it is necessary to pay attention to the condition of the aura and chakras, since it is at this level that imbalances have their source. Healing at the auric level is swift, deep and permanent.

When a chakra is under-energized, there is a shortage of its corresponding colour, which results in difficulty in integrating the positive aspects of that ray. In the case of red, a person will feel tired and listless, lacking confidence, courage and commitment. When a chakra is over-energized, a person generally leans towards the negative aspects of the ray. In the case of yellow, they may become egocentric and controlling. The appropriate colour and its complementary can be used to redress the balance.

There are many ways to increase the flow of colour in your life. Some of these are simple, physical ones. Hence you will find sections on food, interior decoration and clothes. There are also ever-increasing sources of colour available as an enjoyable, nurturing and remedial resource, such as colour baths and colour essences. A list of useful websites is included at the back of the book for reference. Colour can also be used in the breath or in thought, as a support for yourself or another person. The universe is comprised rather less of the solid matter that old science taught us, and more of what the physicists describe as 'quantum soup': energy, information, thought. When you have an image in your mind of a certain colour, this image carries a resonance of the light-ray that is its source. For this reason, corresponding to each of the principal rainbow colours, a visualization is included; an imaginary journey which, in taking you to a land of a certain colour, will fill you with all that you need of that ray. These can be a useful aid in a busy life: a few minutes taken to lie down, breathe deeply and be fed and restored by colour will often revitalize you for the rest of the day; or settle you down for the night.

These are some of the hidden gifts within colour. This vital energy is crucial to our health and wellbeing, our happiness, harmony and fulfilment. Its use as a tool for explaining who you are is the primary focus of this book. Enjoy it!

red

Red is a primary colour: these are ones of simplicity and directness, which cannot be arrived at through the mixing of other hues, and which are also essential to the formation of other, more subtle, variations. The wavelengths at the red end of the rainbow spectrum of light are long and powerful, moving slowly but with great strength. These waveforms are associated with physical energy and heat; those who frequently choose these colours are people of enthusiasm and commitment, passion and warmth. Red is a tonic to a person who is feeling lethargic or depressed, encouraging physical exercise, bringing ardour and courage. This is the colour of raging fires and poppy fields, of red blood and full-bodied wine. It may recall wounds and sores but it also brings to mind the vitality of strong circulation and the glow of warm cheeks. The red ray is outgoing: these are people who like to go out and meet the world. The shades within the red part of the spectrum may range from the deepest scarlets and crimsons to the palest pinks, and lead towards subtle tones such as coral, peach and terracotta, as the eye moves through the rainbow from the red wavelength towards the orange.

# red people

EVERYTHING ABOUT the colour red, and about those who like to have it around them, reflects its power and heat. This is the most stimulating of all the rays. The red person in a state of good health and balance is energetic, enthusiastic, extrovert and physically active. He or she enjoys all that life offers and welcomes any new experience. Red people are action people. They are motivators, with ample energy and the courage to initiate positive change. They enjoy the physical and material aspects of life and are big achievers. They take pride and pleasure in all their endeavours and enjoy the comfort of their material possessions.

Red people are passionate and loving: they may be generous and self-sacrificing; or sometimes quite possessive. Red has a practical and competent character, and is direct in nature: this person calls a spade a spade. Pragmatism, dynamic drive and enthusiasm combine in the red person to produce a creative, original energy for all of his or her projects. Red people generally have two feet firmly on the ground and feel thoroughly at home in the world. Resources generally come to them easily: their strong presence draws people, making them comfortable in many different situations. The red essence is out-going, leading to a strong, and courageous personality, and its revolutionary nature can often provoke change for the better. A red person is never stuck for ideas and her optimism rarely runs dry. Red people often say what they think when they think it, they rarely brood on negative thoughts or hold grudges.

Red is bountiful and thinks big, never doing anything by halves. This sharpens an appetite for healthy competition. Red people, however, can be very stubborn, if this tendency goes unchecked it may not only limit a person's efficiency at work and rebound in their relationships but will also prevent them from enjoying new experiences. The red energy is immediate and spontaneous, although red may sometimes act before she thinks, which can get her into trouble. The colour carries a tendency to be over-impulsive, and also impatient. It is easy for the person on this ray to react quickly to whatever stimulates, or sometimes annoys, him. Think before you speak! Look before you leap!

The red enjoyment of the world and what it has to offer flips over to the negative side, when a person becomes over-absorbed in money, possessions and all worldly demands. The red person has the capacity to be master of the material world, but may suffer the temptation to become its slave. The competitive streak that is part of the red character may also need to be watched: what starts as a healthy focus for achievement can sometimes become careless or destructive. The phrases *seeing red* and *red rag to a bull* have not arisen by chance. The colour red has to do with emotions such as anger and feelings of frustration, resentment or violence. Aristotle said:

> *'anyone can become angry – that is easy. But to be angry*
> *with the right person, to the right degree, for the right purpose,*
> *and in the right way – that is not easy'.*

Frustration, anger and resentment are closely linked to the red character. Red people have a tendency to resist the flow of anything they see as an obstacle in their path; and resistance energizes what we dislike, bringing these things back with more force. Acceptance and thoughtfulness have more power than reaction. The reactionary nature of the red energy may sometimes lead to a person becoming a stick-in-the-mud, rather than the powerful motivator that he might be.

# red flowers, oils and gems

RED POPPIES SYMBOLIZE the sacrifice of lives offered to save others, the stark poignancy of life renewed on the field of battle. Red roses make a declaration of romantic, sexual love. Red flowers of all kinds are an ideal source of red energy in the house and garden, as the colour is strong and often works best in small amounts. Red roses and carnations inside the house; large poppies, red-hot poker, red paeonies and gladioli in the garden.

For flowing energy and instant relief of stress, use vetivert essential oil in a massage base, or add a few drops neat in the bath. Essential oil of patchouli, added to massage oil for the lower half of the body, stimulates energy and cell regeneration, and for many people, if they like its pungent smell, it can act as an aphrodisiac.

Ruby is a precious stone that symbolizes lasting love, abundance, commitment and strength of body and spirit. It connects you with your bloodline, encouraging a spiritual understanding of past and present.

Garnets encourage a person to come out of her shell, stimulate the circulation, balance the sexual energy and boost overall energy and success. They also stimulate spiritual awakening.

# red health and healing

RED INFLUENCES THE lower part of the body from the base of the spine down to the feet, and including the hands. Red people usually have high physical energy and vitality and good circulation. Red energy supports the reproductive organs and the adrenal glands, it stimulates the nervous system and the movement of blood, strengthens the bones and encourages the constant renewal of healthy cells. The choice of red can indicate a need for the ray, when a person is short of this vibration they may display varying symptoms such as tiredness, coldness, impotence or frigidity. Those with wounds, severe eczema, anaemia, poor circulation, cramps, frail bones or a lack of energy and enthusiasm need an increased intake of red energy.

Where the imbalances are physical, food and fruit juices are helpful and immediate sources of the necessary red ray. They can be supported by other, direct methods such as red bath water, auric essences, essential oils and flower essences (see Websites). A boost of red, given in any of these ways, or through visualization, will also help to renew your vitality after episodes of illness, or of sustained over-activity.

Red people, being highly active, physically-oriented, and often in a hurry, are prone to bumps and accidents. They can be in fight or flight mode more of the time than they realize. The complementary colour green, administered through your clothes or surrounding you in the home or workplace, will counteract this tendency by enlarging the feeling of space and time. While red may help to re-awaken a tired libido, at the other end of the scale an excess of red can lead to, or indicate, an over-preoccupation with sex. Blue and violet will help to re-balance the scales by re-directing some of the spare energy to other channels.

# RED symbols

**Red** traffic **light**: beware, **stop**, survive

**Red roses**: romance and **passion**

**Red** lipstick: **arousal**

*Red-handed*: taking another person's **energy** (resources, goods)

**Red blood**: energy, motion, violence, **sacrifice**

**Red flame**: heat, **warmth**, passion

**Red cross**: assistance, aid to **survival**

# RED symbols

**Red** fire extinguishers: beware, **heat**

*Seeing **red***: **anger**, rage

*In the **red***: material energy running low

***Red** letter day*: **happiness** and good fortune

***Red** light district*: **sex** for money

**Rubies**: lasting **love**, abundance, strength

**Garnets**: energy, **circulation**, awakening

# red foods

THE PHYSICAL colour of food is a guide to the nutrients it contains. Naturally-occurring, bright red colour in food is an indicator of Vitamin C, as well as the anti-oxidants beta-carotene and lycopene which play an important role in neutralizing free radicals and protect against cancer. Liver and other red meats are a source of Vitamins E and K, as well as iron and other trace metals such as magnesium and copper. If you are tired or depleted, or subject to frequent colds and chills, red foods will boost your resilience. They also help you to shed weight and are active in drawing toxins from the cells.

The stimulating warmth of red foods is particularly beneficial when eaten early in the day, as they keep physical vitality high. Red energy promotes the healthy renewal of cells and the healing of physical wounds. Red brings vitality to the circulation, the reproductive organs and the adrenal glands, as well as giving an energy boost to the whole system. As the colour itself encourages the appetite, red foods are easy and rewarding to experiment with in salads, fruits, vegetable dishes and in drinks. Red spices have a warming effect.

Red foods will give you a psychological boost, increasing your confidence, courage and drive, and driving away any feelings of listlessness or depression.

Red fruits: strawberries, raspberries, cherries, plums and rhubarb. Red vegetables: tomatoes, red peppers, radishes, red chillies, kidney beans, red cabbage, red onions, beetroot. Red meat: beef, lamb. Red spices: cayenne pepper, ginger and cinnamon.

# red in love

WITH THEIR enthusiasm, generosity and passion, red people can be wonderful lovers. They enjoy the companionship and dynamism of close partnership. In a healthy, well-balanced state red is the sign of grounded and practical people, so they are good at keeping a close friendship warm and alive.

The spouse or mate of someone on this ray will appreciate and enjoy the strength of red as an initiator, and may also need to understand the impulsive and impatient red tendencies, giving their partner the space to cool off from time to time. Red people may need to watch their propensity to be domineering or possessive. And, in a close relationship perhaps more than anywhere else, it is important for the person on the red ray to curb a tendency to speak too soon.

The loyalty and commitment of red people, and their infectious enthusiasm, generally makes their love life – and their family life – fulfilling and fun.

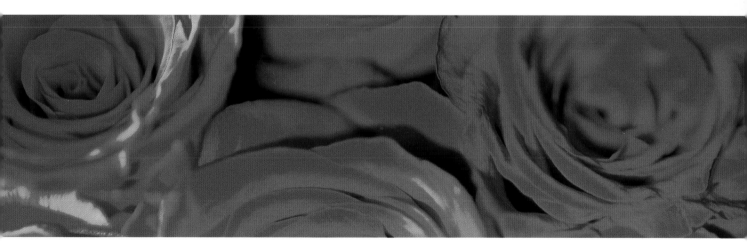

# red parents

RED PARENTS are well equipped for the energetic demands of children and family life, as they enjoy action. Red people are often fun for children to have as parents or carers, as they are good at instilling a sense of enthusiasm into other people's activities as well as their own.

This is all good until it comes to a conflict. The impatience that often forms a significant aspect of the red character may sometimes cause the red parent to be too brisk for a sensitive child.

The red parent is achievement oriented, and will do much to encourage his children's success. When well managed, this produces a good sense of confidence in the child. A parent's red tendency towards drive and competition may need to be watched if it is not to produce a feeling of pressure in a child, and they may need to remember that their own sources of satisfaction may be different from those of their children. Every individual needs to find his own path.

# red children

RED CHILDREN are highly energetic and full of enthusiasm, which is often infectious for those around them. Being natural motivators, they form an invaluable core to any group, whether at home or at school.

Red children are very often initiators – those pro-active youngsters who go out and do things. This is a great gift, but it can also cause them trouble as this red trait is sometimes misunderstood as wilful disobedience or thoughtlessness by those in authority. These children may find themselves taken to task for what they have seen as simply taking obvious or necessary action.

A red child's marked competitive streak generally makes him a strong achiever and a satisfying pupil. He generally enjoys sport and all forms of competition, where he is driven more by the fun of the effort and the game than by a desire to win. The red child may also be hyper-active, and can easily become impatient or feel a sense of frustration with those who fail to see her point of view.

# red in the home

RED HAS BEEN FOUND to raise the physical temperature in a room when extensively used. While it animates and galvanizes, its heavy nature can make it oppressive, so use it with care. This is a good colour to use in blocks rather than throughout a room: large expanses shrink a space and can make you feel restless and impatient. One red wall, or scattered red furniture works well as an energy booster.

Red is a welcoming colour for hallways and reception areas and is useful for warming up north-facing or other cool rooms. Red also works well in the kitchen as it stimulates the appetite. Introduce it in pots, pans and small details, rather than large expanses, if you want peaceful meals. Red is associated with sex but not with sleep. Avoid fixed red in the bedroom if you value a good night's rest; but consider the use of red bedcovers, cushions and candles when you want to make a bedroom more exotic and inviting.

Rich reds suggest opulence, comfort and abundance, as well as liveliness and fun. Red curtains and upholstery can bring depth and animation to a room. Small quantities of red, such as cushions, vases, picture frames and ornaments, enhance living spaces where you like to feel wide awake. Red carpets are too regal for most homes, but red mats are a cheering use of red in a grounding way, especially near the entrance to the house.

# red at work

DYNAMIC, PRACTICAL and pragmatic, red people enjoy seeing quick results. They also like to commit themselves to whatever they are involved in, so once they decide on a job or a project they will want to see it through. Carpentry, engineering, or anything within the construction industry suits red people. So does sport: many red people enjoy working within the field of physical fitness or physiotherapy. Being natural innovators, full of new methods and ideas, as well as competitive, they are well suited to public life and business: project management, sales team-work, or politics all suit the red character.

A red person who likes to work for and around other people might be drawn to a number of high-action jobs, such as an ambulance driver or a surgeon, an aid worker or a fire fighter.

When motivated and occupied, red individuals work hard and efficiently. While they enjoy material comfort, they are driven less by a quest for high earnings than by the great physical and mental satisfaction they derive from a job well done.

# red visualization

LIE DOWN and close your eyes. Take some slow deep breaths. As you breathe inward, feel red light enter your body through your feet, travelling up your legs into your arms and fingertips. Imagine yourself walking through a sun-baked field blazing with red poppies. Run the back of your hand across these flowers and notice their vital, red energy.

Take your attention to your feet and feel their contact with the ground, warm from the summer heat. The movement of the red wavelength is like the rising of the ocean swell, passionate and powerful, travelling with easy grace and strength. It moves toward you from all around, and upward from the ground below. Beneath your feet are earth and soft stones, pummelling and massaging every fibre so the red energy that radiates from them moves through you like warm red wine, nourishing the lower half of your body with the power of this primal ray. Fluid and relaxed, your cells drink and bask in this red light.

When your body is satisfied, let the images recede and take a few deep breaths.Open your eyes, and you will feel energized and restored.

# red clothes

PEOPLE WHO WEAR a lot of red are generally brimming with energy and drive or tired out. If your energy is down, red will act as a tonic and a boost, encouraging physical movement and exercise. It alerts and excites and is impossible to ignore: it helps you to concentrate and to achieve your goals.

Because red helps you to be outgoing, assertive and confident, it is a good colour to wear for business meetings or on occasions when you wish to bring focus and force into your communications. It keeps you on your toes and helps you to be competitive in a healthy and balanced way.

While the colour is stimulating, too much of it can be draining, so avoid the colour if you are easily tired. Red is a supportive colour for anyone who is fit and healthy. For those who suffer from any kind of heart disorder it is not an appropriate colour to wear, particularly around the upper part of the body, as it has the effect of raising blood pressure and quickening the pulse. The same applies to those who suffer from stress or nervous anxiety: Greens, blues and violets are a better choice here. Remember that the colour red can act like a *red rag to a bull:* if you are prone to irritation, anger or aggression, red is best avoided.

# red in a nutshell

DYNAMIC RED ENERGY can bring inspiration and success. Red is the colour of love, generosity and warmth. Know your own strength. Red has a loving nature, commitment, drive, a capacity to keep to goals once set, and great enthusiasm. Let go of a tendency towards irritation, anger or impatience and your life will run smoothly. Use this colour when you wish to:

- Boost your physical vitality, your sexual drive, or your enthusiasm for life.

- Find the courage and the spirit of adventure, as well as certainty, that will enable you to commit yourself more strongly to a person or a project.

- Express hidden anger or frustration in a healthy way, or protect yourself from others' resentment or negativity.

- Overcome anxieties about money and gain increased fulfilment and success in business and work.

- Feel more at home in the world. Gain a stronger sense of where you belong.

- Overcome the resistance you feel to any difficult circumstances in your life, so that you live in the present and find creative ways to alter your future experience.

- Restore depleted physical energy and vitality after a period of over-activity or sustained stress.

- Learn to say 'No!'

pink

The colour pink arises from the combination of red and white. Its nature is in some ways similar to the red colour which is its source, but pink also has its own quality. This is a ray of quiet perception. It is gentler than red, but in some ways it is more intense than its parent hue. Where red may sometimes be loud and direct, the power of pink lies in its quietness and its subtlety. Like red, pink carries great warmth, but where red denotes passion, pink signifies compassion; where red is impulsive, pink is more cautious. If you are a pink person, finding yourself constantly drawn towards variations of this hue, you may discover that you have a little more in common with the essence of red than you thought you had. Pink carries the resonance of that powerful and passionate hue hidden within the depths of its nature. The kindness and warmth of pink is a hidden power and strength that often remains unacknowledged. This is a colour that nourishes and supports, burning negativity and replacing it with the potency of unconditional love. There are many varieties of pink, extending from deep fuchsias to pale coral and peach.

# pink people

PINK PEOPLE ARE sensitive, warm and kind: generous almost to a fault. They have keen intuition. This is man's highest faculty, and makes the person on the pink ray a valuable friend to all those who rely on her, as well as to herself. With their naturally acute perception of the feelings of others, pink people respond warmly to children, animals and to all sensitive creatures. Being emotionally alert, they are also tactful. Pink people are tender and protective, always watching out for those they care about.

The pink person is loving and empathetic. He steps easily into another person's shoes and feels what they are experiencing. The pink energy, and anyone who carries it, has a naturally calming and restoring effect on those around. This person is positive: the pink tendency to be grateful for what is already in one's life, rather than worry about what is lacking, will always ensure that his needs are met, and more.

If you often choose pink, love is all you need. The caring essence of the pink person is the source of their hidden strength, which is often under-estimated by others. In men and women, the feminine aspect of this character is strong: in other words, the pink person is naturally creative and his tendency to nurture – whether this is directed towards plants, people or ideas – makes him fertile and abundant. The imagination in this ray, too, is fertile. Pink qualities produce natural artists of many kinds, with an appreciation of all that is harmonious and a desire to create beauty in their surroundings.

Pink people often need to discover a sense of love, value and appreciation for themselves. People drawn towards this hue are liable to see the needs of others more clearly than their own, and to underestimate their own value and autonomy. This can attract friends and mates who fail to offer the love and respect the pink individual deserves. There is a tendency in the pink person to be over-generous and care should be taken to avoid becoming drained by the demands of other people.

The pink person sometimes lacks realism, viewing people or events through *rose-coloured spectacles*. They may be reluctant to take on the full reality of adulthood, finding it hard to root themselves in the present. The pink character may also include over-sensitivity and a need to protect herself, which can have the effect of alienating those whose company she needs the most. They may also feel too great a need to be liked and approved, which can sometimes prevent a pink person from saying what she really thinks or feels, or may leave her feeling empty emotionally.

People constantly drawn to pink are those who like to please and not to offend. It is often difficult for them to express the real emotions they are feeling, especially when these are negative. They may be burying emotions of anger and resentment, which need to be expressed since suppressed emotions only lead to ill health of one kind or another. It is important for those on this ray to trust their own voice.

Pink people can also feel frail and vulnerable over questions of their value and their ability to earn a good living. They may too easily fall in with the wishes of others, finding it hard to refuse the requests or demands put on their time. They do well to see that no-one can truly assent who has not first learned to say 'no'.

# pink flowers, oils and gems

ROSES ARE ONE of the most ancient aphrodisiacs, as the Romans showed when they strew pink rose petals on the marriage bed. Pink carnations are widely offered as a symbol of lasting love. Pinks, or dianthus, with their fragrant smell, bring a softening energy into any space.

Essential oil of rose concentrates the pink ray in a potent form. It is not only an aphrodisiac but is also supportive emotionally for women or men. Rose oil added to a massage base for application specifically around the womb area is benficial for feminine conditions, but it is also a general muscle relaxant and ideal vaporized or added to the bath.

Rose quartz is a soothing, gentle, feminine stone, which helps to clear fears, vulnerability or the pain of a broken heart. Tourmaline is tranquil and calming, healing emotions and balancing male and female energies to promote greater tolerance and understanding.

# pink health and healing

PINK PEOPLE EASILY give too much of their energy to those around them, leaving them physically as well as emotionally drained. People on this ray need to keep their bodies well nourished with this colour, along with red, peach and orange, to keep their strength up.

Pink is both warming and soothing so it works well as a muscle relaxant. Emotionally warm by nature, pink people may, nevertheless, feel the cold physically. Keeping red around you will stimulate the circulation. Pink people, men as well as women, may suffer from hormonal deficiencies and problems around the area of reproduction. Rose quartz and other pink stones concentrate the pink ray; so does the essential oil of the rose flower. Pink bath products are nurturing and pink bath water can easily be mixed using a small quantity of red food colouring or some colour bath essence (see Websites); spritzers and visualization are also immediate.

Love is the primary healing force: pink works deeply in helping a person to overcome difficulties in their relationship with a parent – most particularly the mother. It also helps those suffering from low self-esteem and feelings of loneliness and sadness.

It promotes self-acceptance and respect, and alleviates feelings of irritation and hypersensitivity. Pink sheets, clothes and furnishings all play an active part in the therapeutic role of this ray.

# PINK symbols

**Pink** wrappings for babies: childhood and **love**

**Pink** roses: romance

**Pink** champagne: **celebration**, gratitude

**Pink** elephant: **unreality**

**Pink** for a girl: **feminine** qualities of intuition and sensitivity

**Peachy-pink** fruits: soft and velvety, easily bruised, sweet and **delicious**

**Rose** quartz stones: feminine, **gentle**, soothing

# PINK symbols

**Coral-pink** gemstones: physical support and **protection**

**Pink** tourmaline: tranquillity, male-female balance

**Peachy-pink** complexion: **health** and **beauty**

*In the* **pink**: general well-being

*Think* **pink**: bring yourself **good** fortune

**Rose-**coloured spectacles: **lack** of realism

# pink foods

PINK FRUITS and vegetables are generally good sources of Vitamin C. They contain red energy in a softened and diluted form, so they are vitalizing and frequently anti-oxidant, particularly in the form of fruits such as melon, watermelon, papayas, plums, fresh figs and pink grapefruit. Sweet potatoes are nourishing and full of energy. Rose water can be a fragrant pink addition to sweets and desserts.

Pink fish and meat sources are easier to digest than red meats. Fish, such as salmon, trout, soft herring roe, shellfish and other seafood are generally mineral-rich, although it is a good idea to know the origin since intensive fish farming and pollution have altered the constituents of some of these foods. Similarly, chicken and other birds offer healthy pink flesh as long as they have led a free life.

Pink fruits: melon, watermelon, papayas, plums, fresh figs, and pink grapefruit. Pink meat and fish: chicken, pheasant, duck, salmon, trout, soft herring roe, shellfish, seafood.

# pink in love

BEING GENEROUS and sensitive, pink people are good at nourishing relationships with those close to them. They also have a great affiliation with romance. It is vital for a pink person to love and feel loved. Pink sensitivity ensures that such a person is well tuned into the thoughts and feelings of those she loves: there is a pink inclination towards hypersensitivity, on the other hand, which can lead to unnecessary tensions.

When she has a partner who appreciates her, there is nothing the pink person will not give. Pink people can feel vulnerable though, and they may put themselves last too often, so they end up feeling like the door mat. They must not be afraid to ask for what they need for themselves: this generally produces a positive response, which comes as a surprise to those accustomed to needless self-sacrifice.

The pink person sometimes has a tendency to put on *rose-coloured spectacles* in romantic relationships. A good dose of realism can prevent the harsh landings that might otherwise come later. If the pink individual does not put too many emotional eggs in one basket, enjoying friendship and family love as well as romance, he will stay in touch with his strongest talents – and be happy.

# pink parents

PINK PARENTS are intuitive and sensitive towards the needs of children, giving them a solid grounding of love and acceptance for life ahead. They are quick to feel what is happening around and inside a child, and to respond in an appropriate way.

Pink people generally enjoy sharing in their children's activities and regard the job of parenting as fun. Many pink parents are glad of the opportunity to re-enter the world of childhood, particularly as this offers the opportunity for a re-living of their own early years, which are always near to the pink person's heart. These may contain a store of happy memories, or unfulfilled wishes that can now be lived out through care for, and enjoyment of, the new generation.

Pink people must avoid the pitfall of total self-sacrifice in favour of others' needs. Pink parents can be over-kind and over-gentle. While love is the essential building block for the raising of any healthy child, the other key word in parenting is discipline. A child will be happier if she also knows the boundaries and the rules. Pink parents are protective and need to avoid becoming over-cautious.

# pink children

PINK CHILDREN are wide open and very receptive to all impressions received. They share the joys of others but also their pains; and they may be easily hurt. They are unwilling to see anything but good in those they like, so that acts of unkindness or disloyalty in their peer group are hard for them to comprehend.

The pink child makes close friends, she is happiest in one-to-one relationships, and is quick to create imaginative games and activities. Such children are affectionate and loyal to their friends.

Pink children may become caught up in the Peter Pan syndrome, loving their childhood and being reluctant to let go and move on. This child may need to be convinced that life in the adult world is not all worry, but can also be fun.

In a safe and loving environment, a pink child will thrive. Impressions in a pink child go deep. They may need more protection than average, but being imaginative as well as suggestible they thrive under encouragement – particularly in all those areas, such as music and the arts, where intuitive gifts are valued.

# pink in the home

PINK CREATES a sense of well-being, harmony and acceptance of oneself and others. In its many tones and tints, pink acts as a declaration of love – romantic or tender. It works well in spaces large or small and the whole range of pink tones harmonize well with green and turquoise.

Pink in any bedroom keeps the atmosphere gentle and nurturing. In the bedroom of an infant or a young child it is calming, relaxing and affectionate. It is worth remembering that while pink is currently thought of as the archetypal feminine colour, it was considered in the nineteenth century to be the colour for small boys. Men and women also respond to the qualities of the pink ray in the bedroom, where it has a beneficial effect on the quality of your sleep and dreams. Bathrooms, too, benefit from pink. It is a warming, comforting and nourishing colour in which to be naked.

Pink light is flattering and the colour fosters feelings of youthfulness. Pink curtains can have a similar effect as they filter natural sunlight. Use soft pinks for walls, curtains and upholstery to create an atmosphere of contentment and peace.

# pink at work

PINK PEOPLE are often drawn towards work that involves looking after others in some way. Preferring one-to-one communication or small groups, they thrive in situations where they make part of a small working group and where their natural qualities of softening and harmonizing can be put to good use. Nursing, counselling or other therapeutic occupations, childcare, primary school teaching, social work and care of the elderly all suit the pink character.

The imaginative skills of pink people, together with their creativity and natural sense of beauty, might well draw them towards the creative arts – interior design, stage set design, advertising or other media work, or any situation in which an artistic flair can be developed. Many pink people love to work with their hands, developing projects or encouraging things to grow.

Being intuitive, observant and highly empathetic, these are good team members in all sorts of occupations where an ability to see beyond appearances to the heart of situations and people makes them an invaluable asset.

# pink clothes

THOSE WITH PINK complexions often have a preference for pink clothing, and also something of a propensity for outgoing activities, but as in all the other areas where the pink personality is evident, they are reluctant to put themselves forward or even to acknowledge their own ability and value.

Pale pink clothing often indicates a person with a warm heart and an open nature, always willing to listen, and reliable as a friend. It can be an indicator that a person feels vulnerable, but it also suggests someone with the generosity and will to put other people first and a reluctance to make demands or draw attention to themselves.

All shades of pink are nurturing. Gentle pinks are soothing and healing for the emotions. To develop confidence, the slightly bolder pinks, such as rose, will help a person to express emotions and develop self-belief. Shocking pink and bright magenta are provocative and sexual: they help in promoting fun. Peachy-pinks help to encourage self-acceptance, and to move a person away from an abusive or one-sided relationship into the give-and-take of a grounded partnership.

# pink in a nutshell

IMAGINATION, COMPASSION and intuitive warmth underpin the happiness of a pink person. Believe in yourself: know and respect your own strength. Be willing to receive some of what you so easily offer to others. Trust your inner voice and be kinder to yourself. Your key strengths are compassion and tenderness. Your key lesson is self-nurturing. Use the colour when you need to:

- Find more kindness and generosity; accept the things you cannot change.

- Encourage others around you to feel more kindness and generosity for you!

- Cultivate a relationship with the mother, or child, or any other aspect of the *inner woman* within yourself. Develop your powers of intuition, creativity and feminine subtlety and grace. Develop an attitude of gratitude.

- Feel more at ease with yourself. Help another person to feel safe, secure and loved. Calm anxiety; restore yourself after a period of nervous tension.

- Soften and nurture relationships in any context, creating a greater sense of warmth and harmony in the home, the bedroom or the office.

- Nurture yourself in pregnancy and early parenthood: this ray will help both you and your unborn baby to feel *in the Pink*. Pink is also supportive in helping you to tune into the needs and the energy of the child you are coming to know, before and after the birth.

- Start to feel young again!

orange

As your eye moves through the spectrum, reds and pinks turn towards the sun. Yellow combines with these colours, introducing shades of coral, terracotta and peach, which in turn become orange. These are rays that offer comfort, nourishment and friendliness. They recall Italian patios and summer fruits, the sensuous opulence of Southern climes, and the softness of warm sand. They combine a reassuring earthiness with the uplifting suggestion of sunshine. Orange rays still offer stimulation and heat but in a more muted form, reminding us of fiery sunrises and sunsets, rather than the intense heat of midday, and the warmth of the fireside hearth. They are at once uplifting and grounding, stimulating and reassuring. Orange suggests strong vitality, physical activity and power, enthusiasm and a natural optimism. Individuals drawn towards these hues are those who both offer and need the warm security of home and companionship, and they also love adventure and exploration. Orange is effervescent and ebullient: the colour prompts you to get up and greet the sun. Orange surrounds all social interaction, emotional bonding and fun, moving fluently between one person and the next. It is a colour that speaks of instinct, ancient wisdom, inner knowing. Like liquid fire, orange glows deep and grows brighter for the sharing of itself.

# orange people

THE PERSON ON the orange ray is warm-hearted and determined, flamboyant and outgoing. Orange people tend to see the best in everything and everyone, radiating joy and happiness. They are natural gamblers, living life on the edge, full of risk and enterprise. Orange people are spontaneous – always ready to respond to the moment, full of ideas, enthusiasm and fun – but they are also capable of patience when this is required, and have subtle, intuitive skills. They have high vitality, both physically and emotionally; their *joie de vivre* and infectious enthusiasm bring heart and soul to any social gathering.

Orange people have insight and understanding – an ability to see the heart of whatever person or situation they encounter. They are empathetic and sensitive, with ready access to their feelings as the barometer of truth. This is particularly true of those drawn to the paler peach and coral shades of the colour, whose instinctive, insightful gifts play a leading part in their decisions and relationships. The family or core group are bricks and mortar to people close to the orange, coral and peach tones: this strong sense of family and community bonds leads to dynamism and loyalty.

Friendship is vital to orange people, who are orientated towards the two-way flow of loving relationships. They are generally attractive to the opposite sex, they enjoy the company of the opposite sex, and they find great happiness and fulfilment in sexual communication. This high-voltage way of life can make it difficult for orange people to find peace of mind when they have to be either on their own, or confined to a period of quiet inactivity. They can also slip into superficial, irresponsible behaviour.

A key lesson in orange psychology is the balance of giving and receiving in relationships. They may become over-dependent on those around them, particularly on a close partner or friend. This can undermine the orange person's autonomy as well as alienating the person on whom they hope to depend. It is those attracted to the paler shades of orange, such as peach and coral, who are most vulnerable to this type of over-dependency. Ironically, it is their very loyalty, when unguarded, that sometimes draws orange people into this surrendering of their sovereignty.

Orange people may need to spread their friendships a little more widely to dilute their intensity. These individuals can be extremists: this affects not only their opinions but also their moods, which can swing from ecstasy to despair in a very short time. Orange emotions run deep: there is a need to ensure the mastering of one's feelings rather than be enslaved by them. When the orange person wishes to avoid the discomfort of unwelcome emotions, he may turn to some kind of addictive behaviour in order to bury the pain. This stores up rather than solves problems.

For many, pure orange is too dazzling in any but small doses. Orange people, always wishing to be active and dynamic, can also be restless, domineering and over-competitive. Those constantly drawn back towards this ray are sometimes suffering from unexpressed emotional traumas or difficulties, which have prevented them from moving forward into the ease and flow of mutually supportive relationships. An attraction towards these rays may indicate that a person is harbouring some kind of shock or trauma from the past, which is preventing him from partaking fully in the present.

# orange flowers, oils and gems

ORANGE FLOWERS, such as lilies, tiger flowers, gladioli and some shades of marigold light up any flower bed. They bring a dash of this inspiring colour into any part of the house and are an ideal gift for someone in need of renewed vitality. Orange-flower water is a useful treatment for acne, as well as having a delicate and delicious aroma.

Orange blossom is an ancient symbol of fertility and joy. It is the source of the essential oil neroli: this makes heavenly perfume, it reduces anxiety and is also an aphrodisiac. A few drops of essential oil of orange or tangerine (not more than 3 or 4 to avoid skin irritation) make a wonderfully warming, winter bath. This is even better blended with a spicy oil such as cinnamon or clove. Ginger and sandalwood also concentrate the orange ray. Add these to massage oil for application around the lower abdomen, to strengthen the digestive organs and immune system, and to process emotional difficulties, or use them for a stimulating and warming massage.

Carnelian stones, which vary in colour from deep orange-red to salmon pink, are joyful and energizing, promoting self-confidence, courage and ambition, and clearing digestive problems. Coral, whose colour also extends across a wide range from peachy-pink and brown through russet to orange, helps in encouraging a person towards emotional independence, and supports those involved in caring for others.

# orange health and healing

ORANGE PEOPLE HAVE enormous vitality and zest for living, which encourages good health. Orange influences the lower part of the abdomen and the spine. In imbalance, Orange people may suffer problems with the absorption of their food – constipation, diarrhoea, yeast overgrowth and eating disorders are among the most common symptoms. The digestion, the spleen and the pancreas are all strengthened by these rays. Where there is under-activity within the digestive system, increase the intake of orange foods and drinks, as the colour encourages movement and fluidity. Where there is physical over-activity or emotional irritation, a calming blue or violet, particularly if this is applied through crystal or aromatic therapy around the abdominal area, is often more helpful.

Orange, taken as food or applied to the skin or the aura, can bring motion back into joints such as hips and knees, where painful experiences have made a person unwilling to move forward with the flow of life. The orange rays cannot be promoted too much for the benefit they bring to the emotions, as they encourage the digestion of all experience, ground your body and raise your spirits.

A strong feeling of attraction towards the colour orange sometimes indicates unresolved shock or trauma – a never-been -well-since syndrome. This colour helps to resurrect buried memories, so they can be healed and released. The spraying of orange into the aura (see Websites) is a fast and effective method, as is a bath soak. Visualization can also work powerfully and fast. Blue placed around the throat will then help in the expression of these memories; and violet, such as an amethyst stone or vaporized lavender oil, will encourage healing.

# ORANGE symbols

**Orange** fruits: **health** and vitality

**Buddhist** robes: **joy** and surrender

**Orange** flames: **glowing** and flowing

**Orange** leaves in autumn: **relinquishment**

**Orange** traffic light: time to **pause**

**Terracotta** sun terraces: **warmth** and good things

**Orange** sunrise: optimism, **new** beginnings

# ORANGE symbols

**Orange** sunset: seeing **deep**, letting go

Peachy-**orange** fruits: soft and **velvety**, easily bruised, sweet and delicious

**Coral**: highly sensitive sea organism, first to react to pollution

**Orange topaz** stones: strength for digestive and sexual organs; immunity

**Coral** jewels: sense of delicacy, **beauty** and strength

**Carnelian** stones: **joy**, happiness, courage

# orange foods

ORANGE RELATES to the sacral chakra, which governs the lower abdomen: it plays a vital part in the digestion of food. Orange foods are helpful in strengthening or treating the colon, the kidneys, the gall bladder, the spleen and all aspects of the digestive system, including emotional ones. The choice of the colour orange sometimes indicates that a person is fearful of moving forward. Orange foods bring comfort and reassurance that provide emotional strength; and their exuberance brings the courage for movement and change. The warming effect of orange spices brings support to those with cold systems and a frail digestion.

The vitality in the orange ray is reflected in Vitamin C-rich oranges. Egg yolk is a rich source of minerals and Vitamin D; and all orange fruits and vegetables are rich in beta-carotene and other anti-oxidants. These also withdraw toxins from the body cells where they are stored. Conversely, those with an existing weakness in the gall bladder should avoid oranges, which act as an irritant to this organ.

As orange is a stimulating ray, orange foods are most beneficial when eaten in the earlier part of the day: they are warming, prompting the body towards action and movement. These foods help to keep the body functions fluid and dynamic.

Orange fruits: oranges, satsumas, peaches, melons, mangoes, guavas and apricots. Orange vegetables: carrots, orange peppers, squash, sweet potatoes and pumpkins. Orange spices: ginger, turmeric and cumin.

# orange in love

ORANGE PEOPLE love to be in love, enjoying the excitement of a romantic partnership, and being generous in love as in all other aspects of their lives. In good balance, they give their all and receive everything. Intimate relationships can be the source of huge joy, but also of devastating despair.

When the orange person is in glowing health, her love life is harmonious, joyful and fun. But when this individual slips out of balance, she may fall in love with someone unavailable, or become over-dependent on the person she is with. Orange people are guided more by their feelings than by the forces of logic. This can mean that at times their emotions are all-consuming. They are easily wounded and it is important for the health of close relationships that the person on this ray communicates openly and honestly about close personal issues.

If your choice is towards the paler shades of orange, where insight and empathy are acute, your lover is fortunate in having so committed a friend who understands so easily their feelings and moods. You may be less good at ensuring that you yourself are always fully understood. To attract someone worthy of your qualities, you may need to put a higher value on yourself.

# orange parents

ORANGE PEOPLE enjoy the warmth of all close relationships, so children are of great importance to them. They love to give, and the children of orange parents will grow up in an atmosphere of abundance. Orange people are tuned into the physical aspect of life. They enjoy food and all good things; they like to touch and be touched. They create an environment in which friendship and affection ares easily expressed.

The orange parent often has an intuitive grasp of what it is to be misunderstood or even abused, so they will take great care to protect the children in their care. They are enthusiastic and energetic, but their natural sense of respect for another person will stop them from being pushy.

Orange parents, especially those attracted towards the paler hues, have a strong sense of group affection and loyalty, which creates firm bonds and family friendship. The commitment of an orange person towards the job of raising their children is deep.

The orange person's natural high spirits and sense of fun are obvious assets in the care of children, but too much orange can be stressful. For security, children also need the balance of peacefulness.

# orange children

ORANGE CHILDREN are active, energetic and curious, as long as they feel safe and secure. They are generally lively and friendly, and fun to be around, so they fit easily into any group, where they often find themselves at its centre. The orange child feels things deeply and has a highly developed intuition. He empathizes with the sadness of others and also shares their joys. It is pointless to attempt to shield an orange child from any difficult situation: he knows more in his guts than many of the surrounding adults have understood.

In order to thrive and prosper, it is essential for orange children to know that they are cherished. Without that assurance, they can be over-dependent or clingy. They may be hyperactive and may suffer mood swings, from extreme excitement to disappointment, or from anger to joy. They live in the moment and are quick to forgive.

The child who resonates with the peachy and coral hues is especially sensitive and impressionable. Care must be taken to protect him. It is important to remember the power of words to encourage and heal, and also to wound. The orange child will respond dynamically to all stimulus, positive or negative, and also to all reassurance.

# orange in the home

PURE ORANGE is such a powerful stimulator that it has been used in factories both to reduce the heating bills and to startle the employees out of taking too much time out in the washrooms! Bear this in mind if you are thinking of getting out some orange paint. Terracotta, amber, burnt orange or rust, peach and coral all contain the warming, radiant qualities of orange without the alarming and flamboyant nature of the pure hue. In the deeper, subtle forms, orange is grounding; in the paler tones it is comforting.

Orange encourages sociability and high spirits, so with careful use it can be an asset in a dining room or other area where people meet. It is anti-depressant, encouraging enjoyment and humour. It fosters exploration and creativity, and stimulates the appetite – for life and for food. As a result, it is good in kitchens. Colour enters our bodies through the skin as well as the eyes. Bath and shower rooms offer great opportunities to absorb the rays we need. Orange, with the related rays such as peach, coral and terracotta are warming, confidence-boosting and optimistic; and they help to clear sad or frightening memories from the past.

Like red, large expanses of orange make a space look smaller, so it can be claustrophobic if over-used. For introspective or sad states of heart, it is a good balancer; for others who are naturally high-spirited, a lot of orange may bring out the negative aspects of the colour, raising stress levels, encouraging over-indulgence and discouraging a sense of responsibility. Bring this stimulating ray into your home in details such as pots and pans, crockery, vases and glass.

# orange at work

BEING PRACTICAL, adventurous and friendly, the orange individual has wide choices. Social jobs suit orange people well: receptionists, disc jockeys and bartenders are often near to this ray. With their natural sociability and their love of adventure and travel, they can equally enjoy life as travel agents, tour guides, flight attendants or within the diplomatic service.

Restaurant work appeals to many on the orange vibration, or other jobs associated with people and food, such as dietary and health advice. As these people are also physically orientated, they are well suited to physiotherapy, massage and other body work, dancing, or teaching yoga, sport or dance. And the gutsy, feeling side of this ray fits a person for creative work in music or art. The bubbling enthusiasm and love of life in an orange person are at the heart of their work.

Those drawn to the lighter, peachy shades of orange are people who bring the qualities of empathy, insight and intuition to their work. They make excellent counsellors. Their creative sensitivity often leads them to handicrafts or media work, especially the dramatic arts.

# orange clothes

PURE ORANGE is an enlivening and cheering colour that lifts the spirits and raises physical energy because of its powerfully stimulating influence. However, it is not an easy colour for many people to wear in quantity or for long periods of time.

Orange is a good colour to help a person overcome feelings of shyness and lack of social ease. Its fluid, warm nature promotes spontaneous social interaction. It also encourages us to become more adventurous and experimental; to dare to leave behind what is safe, predictable and familiar. In this way it promotes independence. The colour lightens people up, banishing seriousness or feelings of despondency, and bringing in fun and laughter.

While orange is flattering and vibrant on those with darker skins, it can wash out paler-skinned people. For many, peach and apricot are more flattering to the complexion and easier to wear, and they offer a similar kind of support to the body and the emotions. At the other end of the scale, rust, burnt orange and deep tones such as terracotta are very warming and comforting. These rich, earthy colours blend easily with brown, gold and other shades of autumn.

# orange visualization

LIE DOWN AND close your eyes. Take some slow, deep breaths. As you breathe in, feel your lower abdomen expand and fill with warm, glowing, orange light. Imagine a stretch of water with the orange sun descending in the sky at the end of a summer's day. Allow yourself to be transported to this scene, watching the sun gently slipping towards the horizon and merging with the water. Feel the warmth of this ray as it spreads through the lower part of your body; notice how the cells respond to its vitality and joy. Watch as this wave runs through your abdomen, its liquid flame warming and penetrating your cells. The orange wave brings nourishment and carries all toxins away. Just as the earth absorbs the warmth of the sun, so orange helps you to absorb the experiences of the day. The colour washes through your body and your thoughts, taking with it the shocks and difficulties of the past, leaving only the wisdom you have gained from your experience.

When you have absorbed all you want of this ray, take a few deep breaths, open your eyes, and wake up to a new sense of vitality.

# orange in a nutshell

YOUR EXUBERANCE and infectious *joie de vivre* are your signature. Trust your gut wisdom. Know your unique value and avoid the trap of over-dependency or the under-valuing of yourself. Your key lesson and strength in love, life and work is balancing the giving and receiving in relationships. Keep the traffic flowing both ways and everyone will flourish. Use orange when you need to:

- Loosen up and bring more freedom into a relationship where one or other of you is too needy.

- Recover from an experience of shock or trauma that has gone deep. Overcome adversity and move forward without fear. Rebuild yourself after a divorce or separation, or detach yourself if you have fallen in love with the wrong person. Attract real love into your life.

- Awaken your sex life: bring more fluidity and spontaneity into your body language and your emotions; become more attractive to the opposite sex; bring greater joy, warmth, companionship and fun into your life.

- Get in touch with your gut instincts and wisdom, perhaps after a period when you have been subject to an overdose of authority from outside. Connect with your inner voice when you feel uncertain about a course of action.

- Break a cycle of addictive behaviour, where the substance on which you felt dependent has not proved good for your health.

brown

Here is a colour that is associated not with the rainbow and sky, but with the earth. Deriving from the mixture of almost any other colours, it nevertheless blends best with the sparkling glow of oranges, yellows and golds, which lift its energy upward from the earth towards the sun. This blanket hue, which accompanies green as the foundation colour of nature, covers many tones from the deepest shades of coffee and chocolate through mid-brown, beige and some of the deeper shades of cream. Brown is the colour of the autumn, the time of year when the natural world goes into recession to prepare for the next round of activity; it is the colour of hibernation. This strong, earthy colour is nurturing. When emotions are running high, or hard to express, brown suggests the protection you may need. Reminding you of firm land and tree trunks, it gives structure and support, offering a dose of common sense. This is the background colour of bricks and mortar, earth and trees; the colour of the seed that transfers its intelligence to the ground, the earth that supports and the leaves whose compost offers nourishment to new life. Brown gives and receives with the cycle of the seasons.

# BROWN symbols

**Brown** soil: **fertility**, stability

Tree **trunks** and **rocks**: reliability, **structure**

**Bricks** and **mortar**: **permanence**

**Brown** leaves: **autumn**, hibernation

**Nuts**, seeds, acorns: fertility, **nourishment**, potential

**Amber** stones: **resilience**, protection, warmth

# brown in the home

BROWN IS NEUTRAL AND safe. Large expanses of this colour can be depressing within a home, but small touches bring comfort and warmth, as well as providing a neutral backdrop to other, brighter colours. The best way to introduce the subtle shades of brown into the home is through natural materials, such as wooden floor boards, quarry tiles and sissal carpets, leather armchairs and clay pots and vases, which reflect the permanence of the natural world. The stability they bring is helpful to anyone feeling insecure. The paler woods, such as ash and pine, introduce brown into the home in a way that is cheering and uplifting; whereas darker ones such as oak and mahogany can have a subduing effect.

# brown clothes

THOSE DRAWN to this colour are practical, down-to-earth and honest people, who like structure and stability. They are patient, but also dislike any sudden change, preferring a way of life that offers a comfortable home and the enjoyment of good food, friendship and safety. This is a good colour to wear when a person feels that these are wanting: if a person lacks mental stability, brown offers a safety net that grounds and secures. It promotes deep reflection and the patience for things to unfold in their own right time. The over-use of brown reflects and encourages the dullness of spirit that fears adventure and change. It also indicates that a person is reluctant to express their real feelings; their essence is buried underground, as it were, and needs to be brought to light.

yellow

As you move onwards from the orange part of the spectrum, your eye will meet the harvest fullness and depth of amber, and then the spring-like freshness of yellow. These amber, gold and yellow hues are the ones that can offer sharp clarity as well as happiness; rejuvenation together with fulfilment. Amber may remind us of the wisdom in the earth; gold of the wisdom of Solomon. Yellow may call our attention to the self-renewing cycle of life, and usher in the joys of spring. This is the colour of laughter and light, optimistic and effervescent – it is a wonderful antidote to any kind of negative thinking. It promotes confidence and self-responsibility. Like red, yellow is a primary colour. Yellow represents the power of the individual will: here is a ray that knows its own strength. Like the colours in the red end of the spectrum, yellow is a stimulating ray, but where red acts as a spur mainly to the physical body, yellow has an activating effect upon the mind. Originality and speed are the hallmarks of this ray. This is the colour of the bright spark, the bulb that lights up at the stimulus of new thought. It is the torch that shines into the dark, seeing the light of a previously-hidden truth.

# yellow people

IF YELLOW, AND ITS close relations amber and gold, are your perennial favourites, you have a sunny, optimistic personality. People generally enjoy being around a yellow person. The yellow motto is to enjoy life, and to see the funny side. This does not mean pleasure at the expense of all else; it means that those on this ray have a great capacity for positive thinking, so they bring an attitude of enjoyment to everything they do.

Yellow is speedy. The yellow ray is strengthening to the mind – the yellow person is the torch holder, who thinks clearly at lightning speed. It is easy for him to think on his feet and live on his wits. The yellow person has a great capacity for assimilating information, for logical and rational thought. Being original and inventive, this person rarely runs out of resources. She thrives on mental challenge and the satisfaction of finding solutions.

In good balance, yellow people are confident and realistic about their own limitations as well as their abilities. They quickly develop self-awareness, which ensures self-control and acceptance of responsibility. With their capacity for decisive and sharp thought, yellow people have a high level of curiosity and a well-developed critical faculty. They have the kind of questioning mind that takes nothing at face value, assuring them qualities of discernment and discrimination. They may not tolerate fools gladly, but neither are they gullible.

The colour yellow relates to the solar plexus, the centre of the ego and the individual will. Yellow people are not afraid to be different. In good balance, they enjoy their own and others' unique quirks and foibles; they have the courage and the clarity to be themselves, to live and let live. They can easily discover in themselves a well-balanced sense of personal power. Being strong-willed and clear in their goals, they are not easily misled, or persuaded to toe another person's line.

The yellow person is often a natural joker or entertainer. No matter how challenging the situation a yellow person finds himself in, he can be relied upon to see the humour – or create it.

Yellow people, being able to access personal power so easily, sometimes need to be on their guard against egotism and selfishness, and the desire to control others. The need to hold the reins of those around is a symptom of fear and its consequence is to drive people away. For all their capacity or potential for clear thought, those on the yellow ray may nevertheless suffer periods of grave confusion and doubt – the darkness before the dawn – when nothing seems to make any sense and decision-making becomes impossible. Yellow individuals can suffer from *yellow belly*: larger-than-average doses of anxiety and fear – sometimes cowardice – which can cause distress and limit their capabilities.

While the person drawn towards the deeper, golden shades of this colour may have something of the Midas touch, they may also be vulnerable to glamour. They need to remember that *all that glitters is not gold*, to use their discrimination in situations where they may tempted by the illusory attractions of glamour, power or wealth.

# yellow flowers, oils and gems

SPRING FLOWERS such as daffodils and primroses are an abundant source of the yellow ray. These are a good reminder of the constant opportunities for spring and rebirth.

Essential oil of lemongrass is very refreshing: a couple of drops used in a footbath to restore tired feet will act as a tonic for the entire body. Like all lemon-scented oils, this is also useful for warding off insects. Yellow calendula flowers are a major ingredient in homoeopathic creams used for soothing inflammations of the skin.

Include lemon essential oil in very low dilutions in the bath – one or two drops are sufficient – or in an oil base for massage, especially around the waist. This stimulates the white corpuscles to counteract infections.

Amber, which is solidified resin rather than a stone, brings the warmth and vitalizing energy of the sun, as well as absorbing negativity, balancing polarities, and increasing resilience. Topaz stones soothe the nervous system, re-energize the body and encourage optimism. Citrine stone is a light-bringing detoxifier which also promotes mental clarity.

# yellow health and healing

THE YELLOW CHAKRA is the solar plexus, just near the navel. It has a large sphere of influence, feeding and supporting the nervous system and the skin, as well as the stomach and many internal organs. This colour and chakra play a vital role in the assimilation of food, experience and information.

Yellow people out of balance can have difficulty in assimilating the more arduous of life's challenges. This may result in indigestion, stomach cramps or other intestinal disorders, or clogging within the lymph system. The cleansing effects of lemon and grapefruit juices will help to clear the lymphatic channels, while the complementary colour violet, worn or rubbed on to the abdominal area, is often a better remedy for digestive tract irritation. Calendula ointment is particularly good for the troubling skin conditions that often arise from an imbalance in the solar plexus.

Yellow people are often highly strung. Yellow and gold help when negative emotions make decision-making difficult. Sun-foods, visualization, yellow stones such as amber, sulphur, topaz or citrine, and essential oils such as lemon, all contribute to the clarity this chakra requires. Auric essences and colour baths, as with all the colours, are also invaluable (see Websites). However, while yellow has the capacity to strengthen the nervous system and the brain, the complementary colours of violet and blue, which have a very soothing and calming effect, are often the best colours for treating anxiety and nervous disorders.

# YELLOW symbols

**Sunshine**: warmth, **light**, freshness and cleansing

**Light bulbs**: intelligence, clarity, **quick** thinking

**Egg yolks** and chickens: **fertility**

**Daffodils** and spring flowers: new **life** and joy

**Lemon** fruits: **stimulating**, astringent

*Yellow belly*: **fear** and cowardice

**Yellow** pages: **fast information**

# YELLOW symbols

**Yellow** décor in **fast food** outlets: speed

**Citrine** stones: clarity of thought, **detoxification**

**Gold metal**: **sovereignty** and permanence

**Topaz**: soothing, **optimism**

**Amber**: vitality, **protection**, warmth

***Gold dust**, heart of gold*: people of great **value**

# yellow foods

YELLOW FOODS play a vital role in the energy system of the body. They are easy to assimilate and digest, providing plentiful sun-energy; they encourage absorption of goodness from all foods; and they help process experience, acting as a tonic to nervous exhaustion and an antidote to fear. Butterflies or constriction in the abdomen respond to yellow foods, which relax the gut, clear the mind, and clean the blood.

All yellow fruits and vegetables are rich in vitalizing, anti-oxidising sun energy. The early and middle parts of the day, when action and vitality are paramount, are good moments to include yellow in your food. The cultivation of new strains of tomatoes, courgettes and other vegetables is making yellow vegetables more prolific. Yellow citrus fruits are high in Vitamin C. Both lemon and grapefruit juice support the liver in ridding itself of toxins or an overload of hormones. Both are useful in morning sickness.

Nuts and seeds fall into the yellow category – these are rich in Vitamins B and E as well as iron, magnesium and zinc. Animal sources include butter and egg yolks, which provide Vitamins D and E. Carbohydrate sources include many breads and pastas; and saffron can be added to rice to give it a sunshine-yellow hue.

Yellow fruits: lemons, grapefruits, starfruits, apples, pears, melons, bananas and pineapples. Yellow vegetables: yellow peppers, yellow courgettes, yellow tomatoes, sweetcorn, parsnips, swedes and turnips.

# yellow in love

WITH HIS SUNNY temperament and plentiful resources, the person on this ray is a direct and easy-going friend. The yellow person enjoys sex but interesting companionship comes higher on his list of priorities. The powerful personal will, which is a strong feature of the yellow character, is both its strength and its weakness: yellow people are fun and interesting but they can also be intolerant and easily bored. The yellow person out of balance easily becomes controlling or egotistical: these are the most common causes of stress within relationships that include a yellow partner.

The ready intelligence of yellow, however, comes quickly to hand in the context of close relationships. She is quick to face and address difficulties and to restore any lost happiness and harmony. The independence a yellow person likes for herself is also easily extended to her friends or mate; and yellow people move on too quickly to hold grudges. If it comes to a split in a partnership, they are better than most at keeping ex-partners as friends.

The independence and resourcefulness of yellow people ensures that they rarely feel lonely; and their radiant sun-energy provides them with plenty of choice in friendship and love.

# yellow parents

YELLOW PARENTS are imaginative and resourceful. Lively and full of ideas, they like to offer plenty of stimulation to the children in their care. As natural students and teachers themselves, they automatically encourage their children to learn and grow. They like to spend time in helping children to understand how things work.

The sunny optimism of a yellow person in good balance ensures that the yellow parent is able to provide an atmosphere in which a child develops curiosity, personal power and self-belief. Yellow people also like order and clarity, where everyone knows the rules. Their children will therefore have a well-structured environment in which to grow up.

When the yellow parent is suffering the confusion, self-doubt, or anxiety that besets her from time to time, a little of this may rub off on her children. At such times the yellow person tends to display impatience and intolerance of others, or the over-control that prevents a child from expressing himself freely. And yellow people may trample over others when something is absorbing them deeply, but if they do, their empowered child will probably soon let them know.

# yellow children

YELLOW CHILDREN are quick, *bright sparks*. Having a marked degree of curiosity, they are always asking questions. They are fun to be around and stimulating to those who have the care of them. Being sunny by temperament, yellow children are often popular. They have a natural sense of their own power; this ability to create the experiences they enjoy keeps yellow children vibrant and optimistic.

The yellow child works quickly and efficiently, enjoying the challenge of mental work. Such children generally know what they want and are quick to focus on their desired goals. He tends to live very much in the moment and his keen excitement may sometimes lead him to behave in a way that appears to ignore the needs of other people. This trait may get the yellow child into trouble, when she has had no intention of hurting others, but has simply been fully focused on the occupation of the moment.

Yellow children out of balance may be nervous and highly strung, sometimes over-competitive and strongly driven.

# yellow in the home

YELLOW IS THE brightest of all the colours, and the nearest to full sunlight. Because of its cheering, uplifting quality, the various modifications of this strong primary colour can be widely used around the home or office. It is welcoming and warming, like sunshine in summer. Pure yellow, however, encourages the controlling, contentious aspects of this ray. Where orange embodies warmth and social interaction, yellow promotes individuality and the self: too much of this ray will encourage arguments or ego inflation.

Soft creams incorporate the yellow energy and also mollify it: this is a good colour for almost any part of the home, and will blend easily with other hues. The deeper yellows, such as amber and gold, can be used in measured quantities to bring in the warming, confidence-boosting qualities of this colour.

Yellow represents and reflects the light of day: it is a good colour in bath and shower rooms for waking in the morning. It also encourages rational thought, making you decisive and clear-headed, so it is helpful in a study or a library.

The happy nature of this ray, together with its stimulating quality, is good for children in daytime. Yellows and golds are warming and appetising in kitchens and dining rooms. The liberal use of lighting brings in the yellow ray in a positive way: we see light bulbs as mini-suns. Yellow-flowering houseplants have a similar effect.

# yellow at work

YELLOW PEOPLE think on their feet and live by their wits – or even their wit. They can be comedians as well as thinkers. With the strong individuality that marks the yellow person out in a crowd, she enjoys a challenge. Yellow people are suited to many mental occupations from research work or teaching, to accounting, city dealing and legal work. They are thorough as well as quick: yellow people make good book keepers or computer programmers as well as psychologists or detectives. If a yellow individual is drawn to creative work, this is likely to involve logical and structural skills, such as graphic design, town planning or architecture.

The positive thinking and humorous nature that characterizes the yellow person makes him a great team member. In good balance he is an excellent administrator; in imbalance he may need to watch a tendency to impose his strong will on others, and to remember that listening and responding to others are as necessary as thinking and taking action.

The mental curiosity inherent in yellow thrives on opportunities to learn something new. Yellow people enjoy running their own businesses, or any situation in which the challenges are mentally stimulating ones.

# yellow clothes

YELLOW CLOTHES are cheerful and uplifting, promoting self-assurance and decisive action. However, this is not a colour that all of us can easily wear. Whereas deep russets and other autumn colours are flattering and warming, it is only those with yellow tones in their skin who are able to wear pure yellow. Without these tones, this colour tends to make a person look unhealthy.

If you feel the need for yellow but find the colour unflattering, golds and ambers are often better choices. These, along with some of the brown spectrum of colours, contain the warmth of the orange range. The yellow shades encourage logical thinking, optimism and self-belief. Yellow clothes and gold jewellery combine to create vivacity and radiance. They are also empowering, encouraging the ability to communicate your intentions. Golds and yellows offset dark and black clothes, which together form a smart appearance that works effectively in a business setting.

The yellow ray will boost the confidence of those who suffer self-doubt, but extensive use of this colour in your clothes, as in the walls of your home, should be avoided by those who know that they have an egotistical, greedy or argumentative streak.

# yellow visualization

LIE DOWN and close your eyes. Imagine yourself lying in a sun-filled garden full of yellow, springtime flowers, breathing in the sounds and scents of spring. See your navel as a large yellow flower, whose petals are opening to the warmth and light of the sun. Imagine in your mind's eye the radiant sun in a cloudless sky, and feel its warm rays as they beam towards you. As you breathe in the refreshing quality of the yellow ray from the sun and the surrounding air, feel the sunshine energy as it caresses the petals of the flower at your navel, opening it to its fullest light. Yellow brings clarity and light to your nerves, clearing anxiety and confusion. The yellow ray softens what it touches, unravelling tight places, clearing dross and making all the inner pathways bright and clean. It fills you with confidence and certainty, giving you the courage and the clarity to be yourself. Feel the happiness of the new life that surrounds you in the season of fresh growth; fill yourself with the joys of spring.

When you have absorbed all that you need of the yellow light, take a few deep breaths and open your eyes.

# yellow in a nutshell

QUICK WIT, self-reliance, personal power and fun are your hallmarks. Maximize them. With your wide-ranging abilities, you may be spoilt for choice: don't dither, just go for it. Cultivate the art of trust and faith if you want to avoid aggravation and stress. Your nerves are there for caution, not panic. Your key strength in love, life and work is self-responsibility. Remember that whatever you are experiencing, you created it, and you have the power to alter it. Bring in more yellow when you need to:

- Increase your confidence and belief in yourself and your value; stimulate and speed up your thinking processes; and trust your individual voice.

- Overcome anxiety and confusion in order to bring clarity and focus into important decisions. Assimilate and metabolize some of your more difficult experiences that may have got stuck in the head or the gut.

- Feel the fear and do it anyway.

- Calm general anxiety and nervous tension, and bring sparkle and animation back into your life. Stimulate and cleanse your body back into physical action after a period of sickness.

- Work hard for an exam or other mental project, prepare for an interview or the start of a new job.

- Have more fun!

green

Green is the colour that occurs at the centre of the rainbow: it is the fulcrum at the centre of the scales; a colour of harmony and balance. It extends from the lime and olive shades that emerge from the colour yellow, and moves through emerald green and into turquoise as the spectrum continues towards blue. Green is the colour of nature and nature lovers, a reminder to us of the beauty and the spaciousness of the natural world. This is a colour associated with spring and new growth: it offers you renewed opportunities and space; it helps you to find a sense of direction and truth, balanced judgement and discrimination. It is the wheel of fortune, the natural cycle of nature that invites the user to be in the right place at the right time. This ray is neither cold nor overcharged with heat. It is soothing and comforting, temperate and even-tempered, blending well with other colours and all people. Green is nature's reliever of stress. This is the ray of tolerance and fairness of mind. Grounded in the earth and looking towards heaven, green is tuned to the panoramic view that fulfils the laws of perspective and balance.

# green people

GREEN IS THE COLOUR that relates to the heart and to the qualities associated with the heart – honesty, generosity and truth. Green people have natural tact and social skills, being aware of and well tuned towards other people's needs. If you find yourself drawn towards the colour green, you are a friendly and outgoing person with a relaxed nature that puts other people at ease.

Green people are tolerant, generous and open-hearted. They are guided more by the truth of their feelings than by the cool logic of reason. They feel easily for other people and are quick to share their time and resources with them. Those on this ray love and respect nature and all things natural: children, pets and plants will flourish at the touch of their *green fingers*. A green person often has an instinctive desire to conserve the resources of the earth and the beauty of nature. Green politics reflect these green concerns.

The green person, being naturally tuned in to the cycles of nature, also has an awareness of the limitations of time, so he or she values it as a precious commodity, generally managing to use her hours well rather than fritter them away. She may also notice a lucky tendency to be in the right place at the appropriate moment. This is a gift associated with trust: notice it and it will grow stronger.

Green represents discrimination, broad vision and truth. Green people are good at seeing all sides of an argument, but this will not tempt them to accept compromise at the expense of the truth. They are great searchers, dedicated to authentic living, but when green energy is lacking and their energy falls out of balance, they may lose their sense of direction – they fail to see the woods for the trees. And while they are natural seekers, they can also be cautious by nature: a need for green may at times suggest a problem with trusting others. But this issue is generally rooted in a buried fear of trusting themselves.

Decision-making can cause the green person agonies of stress, for green people can easily see all sides of an issue. While this is an obvious diplomatic skill, there are times when it may lead to a difficulty in making firm decisions or forming clear opinions: a green person sometimes prefers to balance himself precariously on the fence, attempting to keep all parties happy. At the other extreme, where there is an excess of green energy, he can be moralistic and self-righteous.

In good health the person drawn towards green has a clear sense of direction and a healthy respect for other people's boundaries as well as his own. When there is a shortage of green energy, a person will lack clear goals or a sense of purpose. Without a sense of motivation, they may flip over into laziness and inaction. They may also seek emotional food, encroaching on the boundaries of those with apparently greater energy and resources.

People are sometimes described as *green*, implying that they are naïve and inexperienced. The other side of this is that a person in this state comes without preconceptions to a situation and has a fresh, sweeping view. He sees without prejudice the totality and the full truth of what is before him.

When green energy is in full flow, this person is deeply centred and balanced. When there is a shortfall, the *green-eyed monster* may appear: a green person who has not learned to ask for what he needs for himself may slip into feeling *green with envy* or jealousy towards others who appear more fortunate.

# green plants, oils and gems

NATURE'S GENEROUS supplies of greenery provides endless choice for those in search of this colour. Walks in the park, the countryside, or anywhere that has grass and trees will nourish anyone with a need for balance or restoration. Cultivate an indoor as well as an outdoor garden, no matter how small your domestic space. Even a Bonsai tree brings in some green energy.

Pine and melissa oils are useful in the treatment of the heart and its emotions, but they can cause skin irritation so vaporization in an oil burner is best. Bergamot soothes anxiety, lifts depression, feeds the skin and is thoroughly refreshing.

Emerald gemstones were once used to heal infections such as the plague. They are strengthening for the heart and the emotions, and they promote honesty, self-discovery, fertility and growth. Jade also helps in supporting the heart: it is a stone of friendship – soothing, balancing and encouraging tolerance. Malachite is a good anti-depressant, clearing illusions, supporting eyesight and strengthening positive emotions.

# green health and healing

THE COLOUR GREEN influences the whole of the chest, including the lungs and the heart. In general green people have a great need for green grass and open spaces. Falling in the centre of the spectrum, it is the most restful colour for the eyes, and so provides relaxation for the whole body. It helps to lift people out of time-based pressures and is a reliever of stress in many contexts. Used in clothing and décor, the colour offers a sense of space to those suffering from claustrophobia and a safety net to those who incline towards the opposite extreme in agoraphobia.

The complementary ray to red, which is often associated with red alert situations of danger and alarm, green is a helpful colour when a person is suffering from shock or fatigue; and it relieves biliousness. Green auric essences and baths, along with the vaporizing of bergamot, melissa and pine all help to calm and expand the energy field.

Green people are sometimes prone to chest infections and other respiratory problems, as well as difficulties with the heart, and thus with the circulation. The heart is both the strength and the weakness of green. Where there are difficulties in this area wear green around the chest and harness the energies of plants and flower essences (see Websites). Green visualizations are also deep-acting.

# GREEN symbols

**Green** leaves: **abundance** of nature

**Grass** and trees: **hope** and renewal

**Green** political parties: **ecology**, care for the world

*Greenback* dollar: **money**, wealth

*Green* behaviour: innocent, **naïve**

*Green-eyed* monster: Green with **envy**

# GREEN symbols

**Green** surgical gowns: the flow of blood, **healing**

**Emeralds**: strong heart, **honesty**, fertility

**Jade**: friendship and **tolerance**

**Malachite**: forgiveness and **truth**

**Green** walls in hospitals: **relaxation**

# green foods

GREEN FOODS are the most vital of all that we eat. Green is the colour of nature: it is the colour that heals, refreshes and restores. Green is the balancing colour between hot and cold, mind and body, yin and yang.

The association of green with nature and open spaces makes this colour supportive and cleansing for the body as well as the emotions. Tumours are the organism's unconscious bid for space: Green foods help to reverse the activity of cells in chaos. Green leaves withdraw toxins from the cells and help to purify the blood. They are highly nutritious, replacing the toxins they clear with rich supplies of vitamins and minerals.

Green foods are therefore beneficial at all times of the day. They combine well with all other foods. Green vegetables, particularly the leafy ones, are rich in Vitamins B, C and K as well as iron. The darker the leaf, the greater the nutritional value.

Green vegetables: cabbages, broccoli, courgettes, beans, peas, green peppers, asparagus, artichokes, green lentils, olives, avocado pears, cucumber, the fresher the better. Green fruits: kiwis, green-skinned apples, pears, limes, green grapes. green herbs: parsley, basil, tarragon, oregano, mint.

# green in love

GREEN IS THE QUEEN of hearts. The green person attracts prosperity and abundance, and loves to share his good fortune with others, particularly those he loves. In romantic relationships and in friendship, green people wear their hearts on their sleeve and make themselves completely available to the person who matters most.

Green people are responsible and reliable and are therefore good at creating securely-based relationships. The green hallmarks of generosity, co-operation and warmth provide fertile ground for strong, loving relationships. Truth and integrity are high on their list of values: this is what they offer and also expect from their mate. Sometimes their *green* trust and naïvete need to be tempered with discrimination before they follow their tendency to open their heart too wide, or they may build walls around their heart after the event.

Because green people are generous with their time, their feelings and their possessions, they receive plenty back from those they care about. The caution is to remember that just as you need space and time for yourself, so does your partner or friend. Warmth is necessary but the green person in search of emotional sustenance can sometimes cause another person to feel claustrophobic within the relationship. For the green person in love, envy or possessive jealousy may be lurking around the corner.

# green parents

GREEN PARENTS have an easy-going temperament which enables them to stay balanced and calm. They are good at standing back and allowing their children to develop in their own way, in their own time, without undue expectations. The green person in good balance always sees the broader picture and avoids getting bogged down in daily irritations or in petty judgements.

The green parent, with his wide-open heart, tends to be easy for a child to talk to. He will always take an active interest in the child's concerns and will also respect what a child thinks and says. He may sometimes have an over-developed sense of caution, which can prevent him from encouraging a child towards activity and independence, or promoting her sense of faith, confidence and trust.

Green people generally find it easy to relax. In good balance this is an obvious asset in a parent. There are times, however, when this person can lack motivation and may swing over into boredom and inactivity.

Having a strong sense of responsibility, the green parent in good balance is well aware of her child's own needs and will also reconcile these with the concerns of others. The child of a green parent tends to grow up with a well-developed social awareness and an easy ability to relate to the wider world.

# green children

GREEN CHILDREN are open-hearted and good-natured, getting along easily with all types of people. They tend to spread their friendships widely. Being honest and open, they are generally liked by both their elders and their peers. A green child typifies the innocence, freshness, open curiosity and honesty which are the hallmarks of this ray. She is amazed and easily hurt if her trust is abused.

A green child is benevolent, wanting the best for everyone. These children will often find themselves placed in positions where their diplomatic skills are in demand as messengers or go-betweens. Their sense of social balance, and their ability to see all sides of a question, are good qualities for bringing harmony to teams and groups. They have a strong sense of fair play and will readily fight for a cause, on their own or another's behalf.

A green child is quick to notice the needs of others and to make space for them. He may sometimes be trampled on by those who take his generosity for granted, so that he finds himself lacking in what he needs. This in turn may lead to an envy of others, or jealousy, in which case he will need encouragement in honouring and caring for himself. Although green children are distressed when met by deceitfulness, there are occasions when their determination to see the best in everyone causes them to deceive themselves.

# green in the home

BECAUSE THIS colour is neither hot nor cold, but sits in the middle of the spectrum, it is ideal for any space where you wish for neutrality and peace. Green offers reassurance. Hospitals quite often use pale green for the walls, as it promotes greater feelings of well-being than the starkness of white. Prisons, too, use pale green: it creates the illusion of space when, in fact, that is exactly what the inmates lack. If you live in a small house and want to expand the feeling of space around you, do the same.

Green blends with all the colours of nature, but can look stark and dull on its own, creating inertia. It is too calming to be suitable in large quantities for rooms where activity is necessary, but it works in spaces where decisions are being made, such as the home office. Its universal nature sets off all vibrant colours, and its complementary colours red and pink stimulate activity.

The spaciousness of green can also be used to create boundaries: in halls and stairways it increases the impression of space between different rooms. Similarly, it is helpful in treatment rooms for therapists, supporting both the client and the practitioner.

Green plants bring the vital energy of this ray into any area where green would be unsuitable in quantity. Their soothing energy can be usefully placed almost anywhere and large plants can be used effectively to break up large spaces or soften harsh lines.

# green at work

GREEN PEOPLE are natural harmonizers and are often willing to work behind the scenes. Because of the strong heart energy that the green person carries, he or she is suited to nursing and social work, teaching, parenting and childcare. Clergymen and counsellors are often lovers of green.

The green person is also gifted with natural social skills. These can make him the ideal diplomat, whether literally or more indirectly, in human resources, for instance, or stage direction. Green people have a natural sense of justice and fair play, which makes them good team workers and lubricators. Their temperance and tolerance, their ability to see all sides of a question and their reluctance to make hasty judgements encourages others to trust their decisions.

The green person is also a naturalist. They often have *green fingers*, which may lead them to life as a horticulturalist, a forester, a landscape gardener or a florist; or even take them into veterinary nursing and medicine.

Job satisfaction for green people comes from giving, caring, creating harmony and including friendship in their work.

# green clothes

GREEN IS THE colour of balance, and it blends easily with the colours at the blue and the red ends of the spectrum. As in nature, it is able to set off the vibrant hues that surround it. Green clothes are especially well suited to those with ginger or reddish colouring, green being the complementary colour to red and pink.

This is a gentle, forgiving colour that calms distress and soothes the heart. As a healing colour it is good to wear around the chest, where it gently stimulates the flow of the circulation, calms and deepens the breathing and alleviates feelings of stress. Green clothes give a sense of space and freedom to the wearer. The combination of blue with green augments the feeling of peacefulness that begins with green. The effect of green clothing is generally calming, although those who normally wear a lot of this colour may incline towards inactivity, in which case the complementary energies of red and pink will bring more dynamism into their way of life.

The wearing of green sometimes indicates that a person is over-cautious and has difficulty in trusting others. This person may prefer to rely on his own judgement rather than to go along with the opinion or the company of other people, and may like to keep within her own space. The warm, sociable hues within the orange range will help such an individual to expand and reach outwards.

# green visualization

LIE DOWN and close your eyes. Take a few deep breaths and sense your lungs and chest cavity expand and flow over with green light. Imagine yourself walking in a forest, surrounded by the succulent leaves of a new spring, the chlorophyll of nature gently unfolding itself before your eyes. As you feel the texture of these leaves, see the life force that comes to earth and offers its vitality through the plant. You are lying in an open field. Feel the texture of the grass that grows beneath you, blanketing you against the roughness of the earth. Around you are large, wide-open trees in full leaf, tall, wide and spacious. The green wave that radiates outwards from the trees and the grass fills the air with a pale emerald glow. It flows through your heart and lungs: the fluid energy of emeralds, malachite and jade, encouraging you to reach out and expand yourself. Your whole body begins to feel heavy as it lets go and sinks into the support of the green grass, trusting the earth, trusting the flow of life.

When you feel replete with the energy of green, take a few deep breaths and open your eyes.

# green in a nutshell

THE EXPANSIVE, warm, outgoing nature of green offers rich experiences in a wide world. Trust your powers of wise judgement and discrimination and follow your truth. Accept and value your gifts and talents and give yourself the space you need. Enjoy nature. Your key strength in love, life and work is balance: body and mind; leisure and work; wisdom and power; feelings and thought. Stay firmly balanced within your own centre and everything else will pull together. Bring more green into your life when you want to:

- Take important decisions involving the heart as much as the mind; or release suppressed feelings.

- Create a feeling of space around you when you feel the need of a little distance from whatever is going on; or overcome jealousy if someone else's 'space' looks like a better deal than yours!

- Soothe and heal a battered heart; breathe more deeply and cultivate a feeling of trust.

- Rid yourself of dogma or conditioning in order to discover your own truth.

- Let go of cycles of behaviour and patterns of thought that are no longer useful – outmoded belief systems, for example, or destructive relationships, or negative ideas about your own value.

- Feel more relaxed.

turquoise

Turquoise evokes the cool, calm surface of oceans in sun-baked lands, and the exotic life that plays freely in their depths. This is the colour that spells expansion and the wide freedom of expression that comes when the heart soars upwards and finds its voice. From the palest aquamarines to the deepest shades of peacock, this part of the spectrum is accentuated around artists and artistry, around all those who find creativity in the expression of their feelings. Turquoise suggests the cool tranquillity of water, the wide sensitivity that connects with other people and other forms of life. It is the colour of telepathy, of the Shaman and Native American art. This tropical tint of greenish-blue is associated with dolphins who live and play, vitally alive in every moment of their day, and with the freedom of movement evoked by exotic birds, butterflies and fish. The turquoise ray resonates with those who have found the freedom and the power of creation that open up before us when we come to know ourselves. Turquoise stones, such as turquoise itself, or aquamarine and fluorite, protect against loneliness and self-doubt, building courage and inner strength. This colour has a soothing and uplifting quality that brings peace to all nervous tension, restoring vitality and freshness, and bringing with it a feeling of optimism and youth.

# turquoise people

TURQUOISE PEOPLE ARE thoughtful, original and creative. They allow their emotions to flow freely and are not afraid to express their feelings. These are frequently people who have come to know themselves well, and through their self-understanding they have found a deep knowledge of, and compassion for, humanity. The turquoise person is open-hearted, with a well-developed sense of responsibility both for himself and others. She cares about world concerns and communicates easily.

It is important for a turquoise person to enjoy their personal freedom. These people feel claustrophobic when their private space is invaded too much: they like to live and will willingly let live. They give generously of their time, commitment, affection and resources as long as their independence is respected. They are good at living in the moment, bringing a positive energy to any project without investing too much expectation in a particular outcome. They intuitively know that the best love is detached.

The need for turquoise may indicate that a person is feeling anxious or nervous, or that she is lonely and isolated, her creativity blocked. It may suggest either the calm that comes before a storm, or feelings of neglect. At times such as these, the use of the complementary colour range of peach, terracotta and other warm rays will help to bring the turquoise person back to her centre and to peace of heart and mind.

Turquoise gifts are well suited to all creative or media work. Artists and writers, poets and philosophers, teachers and inspirational leaders all resonate with this ray.

# turquoise health and healing

TURQUOISE PEOPLE HAVE a need both to feel unfettered physically and also for freedom of expression. When the turquoise energy is out of balance and these conditions are lacking, they may become frustrated, anxious or claustrophobic. Turquoise relates to the upper chest: it is where the feelings of the heart and the thoughts of the head find a meeting place. When turquoise energy is blocked, a person may experience sore throats or respiratory infections, asthma or difficulties with the heart. The use of this ray is helpful in encouraging a person to voice their feelings, rather than cough or splutter, palpitate or stammer.

The colour turquoise also relates to the thymus gland, which plays a vital role in the body's immunity. The colour helps to introduce a sense of calm independence and detachment, which boosts immunity on all levels – mental, emotional and physical.

When emotions are running high and pulling a person downward into a negative state of mind, turquoise is a calming energy that will encourage necessary expression and restore the balance between body and mind.

Like all the colours, turquoise can be brought in through bath water colours, auric essences and gems. There are few foods on this ray; nevertheless this colour energy can easily be transferred to a glass of spring water by immersing a turquoise stone in the water and leaving it in the sun for an hour. It should then be sipped.

# TURQUOISE symbols

**Turquoise** sea: **freedom**, expansion

**Dolphins**: telepathic communication, **playfulness**

**Swimming pools**: **relaxation** and play

**Kingfishers**: hard to pin down

**Peacocks**: **self-expression**

**Turquoise** gems: courage, **fulfilment** and success

**Aquamarine** gems: soothing, calm, **tranquillity**

# turquoise in the home

TURQUOISE IS RECESSIVE – appearing to move away from you, it expands a space. Because of its association with oceans and pools, it is traditionally popular in bathrooms, along with pale blue. Studies, children's bedrooms and rooms for social and family activities all benefit from turquoise. Those who prefer warmth often like to complement this refreshing ray with colours such as salmon pink or peach.

As a wall covering, in paint or paper, turquoise makes a strong statement and care needs to be taken over the details in the remainder of the room. By contrast, this colour works beautifully as an ingredient in the design of curtain material, soft furnishings and other details. Its calming, uplifting nature deepens the breath, relaxing all stress-related conditions and promoting creative endeavour.

# turquoise clothes

TURQUOISE CLOTHES CALM you down and lighten you up. They are gentle, joyful and uplifting, encouraging independent creativity of feeling and thought, enhancing youth and freshness. Being cool, turquoise works best in hot climates or in the warmer months of the year. Its natural complementary colours are peach and terracotta, so it suits those with a tanned skin, or people whose natural colouring contains more yellow and red than blue. Red, blonde and black hair are all highlighted by this colour.

Combined with deep blues and indigo, turquoise is visually arresting; and this blending of your heart qualities with the strong authority of indigo can be an excellent clothes choice to enhance communications in any meeting where decisions must be made. Combined with the warmer colours, it makes you feel nurtured and puts those around you at ease.

blue

Blue is a colour that reminds us of cloudless summer skies and peaceful lagoons. The wavelength of blue is shorter than the red wave at the other end of the spectrum: so short, in fact, that it can appear to move very little, bringing with it a sense of peacefulness. Blue is the colour of divinity and truth; of hearing and also of speech. The colours at this end of the spectrum balance those at the other pole in numerous ways. Where red brings heat and passion, blue brings the cool sense of reason. Where reds and oranges stimulate and excite, blues pacify. Where red raises the blood pressure, blue is calming to all things, slowing the pace and bringing order where chaos may have reigned. Where red is active in a physical sense, the activity in blue is focussed more on the realm of the spirit. Where red strides out to meet the world, blue stays quietly centred and allows the world to arrive in its own time. Blue is a colour of patience, trust and faith. Where the energy of golds and yellows provokes questioning and thought, the blue rays encourage acceptance and co-operation with a higher power that transcends the will of the individual. It is the serenity bestowed by the blue ray that lends those constantly drawn towards these hues a quality of strong, quiet independence and peace of mind.

# blue people

BLUE IS THE essence of tranquillity and serenity, contemplation and truth, testifying that *still waters run deep*. Blue people are quiet, seldom needing to draw attention to themselves. Those with a blue theme in their life are strong and independent people who value peaceful communication, and so create it. The quiet confidence of the blue person makes them someone to whom others easily turn for guidance and strength. The serenity of the blue energy brings others near, like the strong oak tree that draws the birds to nest. The blue person has an authentic sense of style and dignity, which often sets him apart from the crowd.

The reliable character of blue people leads them, without any conscious effort on their part, into positions of authority. Integrity, truth and honour are important to those on this ray. Blue individuals can be direct, honest and clear in the communication of their thoughts, even if their feelings are less easily expressed. This is the conservative character in the best sense: the blue person puts a high value on people, ways of life, and possessions that are familiar to her, and she is protective towards the people in her care.

Blue brings to mind the blue robes of the Madonna and the gentle rays of heaven. Those habitually drawn to blue are people who feel a sense of protection, care and responsibility not just to their nearest and dearest but universally. They are generous in giving service and they are messengers of peace.

The blue person is logical, rational and reasonable in his actions as well as his thoughts. This makes him a reliable friend or member of the family, whom people often count on to make sensible decisions. But blue, like all the other colours, needs to be moderated by the other spectrum hues. Too much blue leads to imbalance. The *true blue* tendencies of these individuals may cause them to hold on too tightly to people, possessions or ways of thought that no longer serve them. It can be very difficult for a blue person to let go of an idea, a person or a worn-out suitcase.

Blue people can also be logical and rational at the expense of more lateral and creative thought. Besides this, they are natural introverts, which sometimes prevents them from the ready sharing and creating of new ideas. Carried too far, this tendency can cause the blue person considerable discomfort. He may, for example, want to opt for the quiet life rather than face confrontation: *peace at any price* is a recipe that stores up difficulties for later. The independence of blue people in good health and balance serves as a great asset; too much blue may lead to a stand-offishness that drives away the people they need the most.

This blue independence can fool others into believing that the blue person really is self-contained and needs no support. Since it is blue people to whom others generally turn for guidance and strength, they may feel that this is a one-way flow. In this situation a blue person suffers from the *blues*, or feelings of loneliness and bouts of depression.

The question of authority can be a problem for a blue person, who may easily resent the idea of relinquishing their autonomy in any circumstance. Blue people often prefer to keep themselves to themselves and to make their own rules.

# blue flowers, oils and gems

THE COLOUR BLUE helps us to remember: blue forget-me-nots, as the name implies, are a flower of loyalty. Bluebells herald the arrival of spring, encouraging faith. Blue cornflowers are the colour of full summer and clear blue skies. Other blue flowers include campanula, chicory and lavender.

The striking blue flowers of the chicory plant are used in flower essences. The soothing, calming properties of this flower have a subtle power, helping a person to let go of emotional pain and move towards forgiveness and love. The essential oil of lavender is retardant, soothing and antiseptic. It is also an effective remedy for pain and its relaxing properties promote a peaceful night's sleep. It may be vaporized, added to massage oil or the bath, or applied directly to areas of pain.

Sapphires encourage devotion, self-control, truth and wisdom. They stimulate us to follow our destiny and reach for the stars. Blue lace agate is a light blue stone that protects and stabilizes, calming the mind. Larimar, another pale blue gem, lifts the energy of love to greater dimensions, bringing forgiveness and acceptance.

# blue health and healing

BLUE REFRESHES and soothes, bringing relief to any inflammation, slowing the blood pressure, calming the head and the heart. Blue is connected with the throat chakra which relates to the neck, the thyroid gland and the throat. This is where both the heart and the head find expression.

The calm, peaceful nature of blue is its strength, preserving the blue person from the hyperactive stresses that often beset those tuned to the hotter rays. Reluctance to speak out may cause throat constriction in the blue person. Sore throats, or a tendency to cough rather than to let go and say what you need to say is a common blue trait. A blue necklace or scarf worn around the throat can help a person to speak their truth without fear. A blue visualization, flower essence, blue spritzed directly into the aura, and blue bath water all provide deep-acting and immediate methods to imbibe this ray (see Websites). Lavender oil, vaporized or sprayed in diluted form, is a great soother at bedtime and is also helpful for children who are distressed or teething.

Blue people tend to be thinkers rather than doers. Their systems are cool: they may suffer from low blood pressure, poor circulation, and from chest conditions such as asthma. Blue people need the stimulation of the hotter red and orange rays, which warm the physical body and also counteract the blues.

# BLUE symbols

Blue lagoon: **peace** and tranquillity

Blue sky: heaven and **serenity**

The **Blue** flower: **Forget-me-not**

**Blue** Madonna: universal **motherhood**

*The **Blues***: **sadness**, depression

***Blue** movies*: **observing** rather than living

# BLUE symbols

**Blue blood**: loyalty, authority

**Sapphires**: **devotion**, destiny, beauty, truth

**Blue agate**: **balance**, stability

**Larimar**: divine **love**

**True blue**: conservatism

**Blue collar** worker: **service**

# blue foods

THERE ARE MANY ways in which the colour blue opposes and balances the energy of reds and oranges. The blue ray is soothing and peaceful. Where red foods are stimulating, energizing and expansive, blue is the colour that retracts and slows the pace. Blue foods are good for the later parts of the day, especially the evening, when the body prepares to shut down and rest.

Blue has stronger associations with the mind than the body, so the blue foods that nature provides are limited. They can be useful in calming inflammatory conditions, reducing fevers and neutralizing bacteria. Sore throats, teething troubles, skin irritations and sores all respond to blue.

Blue foods, encouraging the body to be still and conserve its resources, also help those who need to gain weight. The most potent action of this colour is on the mind: blue foods are good for treating headaches, insomnia or general anxiety.

Most seaweeds contain blue energy, and are also rich in minerals. Blue is not a colour that stimulates appetite and too much of it has a depressing effect. Green foods, which are calming for the body, blend well with blue ones to make a peaceful and appetizing meal.

Blue fruits: blueberries, boysenberries, bilberries and blue plums. Dried fruits: raisins, prunes. Blue vegetables: asparagus, seaweed. Blue herbs: blue sage, marjoram, valerian.

# blue in love

THE BLUE PERSON is measured and thoughtful in his relationships. Impulsiveness is not for those on this ray. In love as in other areas of his life, this person proceeds thoughtfully and with attention. When a blue mind decides on a partnership that will work, the rest of her will follow; with her peaceful, strong, independent energy she will co-operate well with her chosen partner. A blue mate is a gift for anyone who values fidelity, integrity and honesty and who seeks those qualities in a partner.

The intimate relationships of a blue person thrive not on excitement and novelty but on mutual understanding. Blue people become more passionate, not less, as they get to know their partner better. Communication is a potential blue strength but the lack of it may be their weakness. It is important for a blue person not to be too controlled about expressing his feelings or he may appear cooler than he really is.

Blue people are observant. The blue lover or spouse treats his partner with respect and is aware of her needs. It is important that his mate is similarly aware of the blue need for times of solitude and peace, which is his vital mental food. Given the periods of respite that are essential for the blue spirit to thrive, this person will be a loyal and devoted lover and friend.

# blue parents

BLUE PARENTS are strong, peaceful and firm. They encourage children to communicate clearly in order that peace may reign. They also foster independence in their children. Blue people are generally good listeners, so the parent on the blue ray can make a good companion and friend for a child.

Blue people avoid the hazards of cosseting and over-protection; but there may be times when they need to remember that for a child love is not always taken for granted but must be expressed. The blue parent in good balance will complement a healthy discipline with plenty of love and care. It may sometimes be important for a blue person to remind herself that the latter is as important as the former, particularly at times when the demands of parenting compete with the natural blue necessity for order and tranquillity.

The air of peacefulness that generally surrounds a blue person in good health and balance can create an atmosphere in which the child's potential will easily blossom. While the colour blue is more passive than the red end of the spectrum on a physical level, the blue mind and spirit are highly creative. This person has the capacity to nourish and cultivate every creative gift of the child in her care.

# blue children

BLUE CHILDREN are strong and independent, and may be loners. Their mental ability is generally high, so that education is easy for them. Their thinking processes may not be the quick ones associated with yellow, but they are deep. The blue child is not only peace loving but also a creator of peace. Where there is conflict, it is often the blue child to whom others will turn for justice or a soothing balm.

A blue child in good balance will easily speak his mind. He has a gift for the clear and lucid expression of his thoughts. He may be less gifted than the red or orange child in the areas of sport that breed instant popularity, but the mental confidence of blue children is high and they are not over-concerned or anxious about what others may think of them.

A blue child who has not yet found his strength may suffer the opposite extreme and have severe difficulties with speech, in which case the colour blue is often a potent remedy to enable him to find his voice. Blue children are thoughtful and cautious, but once committed to any course of action they will follow it through. They form loyal friendships and close bonds with both their teachers and their peers. Once recognized, they easily assume positions of responsibility and leadership.

# blue in the home

BLUE IS ONE of the most restful rays to live with, and very unobtrusive in the paler forms, as it provides a backdrop similar to the one provided in the wider world by the sky.

Blue deepens the breath, relaxing the muscles as well as the mind. It slows the blood pressure and calms the pulse. As a result pale blue is an ideal colour for rooms used for relaxation, particularly after a day of mental work. It is also good for children's bedrooms, encouraging creative work, play and restful sleep. It works well in libraries and study rooms, and also in spaces used for quiet times of prayer or meditation.

Blue is traditionally popular in bathrooms, for its associations with water and the sea. As colour is absorbed through the skin, the bathroom is an ideal place for the ray that any individual needs the most. If calm tranquillity is what you seek, a blue bathroom can be wonderfully reminiscent of a clear sky and a blue lagoon. If you enjoy a warm soak, it is better to look at the other end of the spectrum.

Because this colour can easily have a chilling effect, blue is best used where there is plenty of natural light entering a room. Without it, blue can be depressing as well as cold. Its complementary colours from the orange range, including tones such as terracotta and peach, blend well with this colour and bring in the warmth that it lacks.

# blue at work

BLUE PEOPLE are orderly, calm, independent and strong, with a gift for clear communication. The blue mentality lends itself to a variety of occupations: she may be a business person or a banker, a politician (most likely a *blue* one), a spiritual leader, a corporate chairman, a teacher. Blue people are suited to professions where their natural sense of style, peace and order draw people towards them, making others feel comfortable and safe.

The blue conservationist tendencies might draw this person towards archaeology, history, museum work or art galleries. Blue people also have a strong sense of service. The blue uniforms of nurses and policemen, and the universal *blue collar* of the hard core worker symbolize the willingness of people on the blue ray to dedicate themselves to what is useful. Blue people are also drawn towards overseas development work.

Hard work has its rewards. Blue is the colour upon which others lean, and it is common to see a blue person rise with ease through the ranks from the shop floor to a position of management. It is natural for blue people to take on responsibility and their influence flows smoothly around them.

# blue visualization

LIE DOWN, close your eyes and take some deep breaths. As you breathe inward, see a pale blue light around you, gently brushing the surface of your skin and the membranes of your nose and throat.

Imagine yourself floating on the warm surface of a blue lagoon. The stillness of the water reflects the cloudless sky above. Blue is the colour of protection, of tranquillity and peace. It is also the colour that brings fluency and strength to all that you wish to say. The pale, heavenly light of the blue ray moves through your nose and face, caressing your neck and shoulders, bringing with it a feeling of stillness and calm. The colour breeds confidence, trust and faith. Allow this gentle light to soften all that it touches, so that your thoughts and the words you wish to say become gentler and clearer. Energy blocks dissolve as the blue wafts through you, to fill every cell of your body with the feeling of peace that is the colour blue.

When you have received all that you need of this ray, take a few deep breaths and open your eyes.

# blue clothes

BLUE IS CHOSEN more than any other as a colour for uniforms. The blue worn by nurses, the police force and the navy signifies loyalty and the ethic of service. They also send out a message of peace and care underpinned by authority. The blue jeans worn by teenagers and young adults since the 1960s give young people a sense of belonging. For the same reason, blue clothes are often worn in a corporate setting. If you are attending an interview or partaking in a conference, blue is a likely choice and a good one: it shows a sense of responsibility and independence tempered with loyalty. It also encourages clear, honest communication.

Blue is a protective and soothing colour. It supports anyone suffering from stress, when they need peace and relaxation, or when there is a need to withdraw mentally from pressures that may still surround them physically, such as in a busy office. It also encourages strength and self-reliance: it helps a person to access their sense of personal authority as well as keeping them tuned into their responsibility for others.

Too much blue has a depressing, cold effect. A shirt or scarf of its natural complement from the orange range immediately balances the energy, bringing warmth and cheer.

# blue in a nutshell

STEADINESS, TRANQUILLITY, independence and peaceful communication: these qualities mark you out from the crowd. It is easy for you to stay cool – but don't stay too cool. Your calm strength draws people towards you. Cultivate your latent powers of communication to ensure that people listen to you as well as talk. Your key strength in love, life and work is a peacefulness based in confidence and faith. Use blue when you need to:

- Feel stronger and more independent, and know your own mind; communicate peacefully, especially over something that may be hard to say.

- Feel protected and nurtured, particularly during times of change, and develop a deeper sense of faith and trust.

- Calm over-activity of any sort: in the mind, when there is too much thinking, or in the body, when there is pain or soreness anywhere.

- Overcome feelings of loneliness and depression: cure the *blues*. Find your voice, overcome shyness or reticence and speak out. Encourage yourself to let go of things or habits that you have held on to for too long.

As day turns to night, the sky moves from a clear pale blue to the deepest indigo. This dark blue takes your understanding of the universe to new heights and depths. A hint of the passion and power of red, buried within the depths of this inky colour, gives this ray a more complex and mysterious nature than that of its more straightforward blue relation. It is a royal colour that brings to mind the sovereignty of kings and queens, the authority that comes with knowing oneself. Indigo is a colour that reveals the vastness and the oneness of the universe: the moon and the stars, that may seem so remote by day, uncover themselves in the indigo colour of the night-time sky. This deep-blue domain is the land of inspiration and dreams. Indigo is a colour that lifts the veil from your eyes, encouraging you to see beyond the illusions of the physical and the tangible world. From the depths of its darkness, it brings flashes of inspiration. This colour helps you to explore the world of the imagination, of the unconscious; to discover the muse – the source of creative endeavour within your own life – and thus to become master of your destiny. Seize the gifts of the indigo ray and it will set you free.

# indigo people

INDIGO RELATES to the brow and what is often referred to as the third eye. This is a colour of great penetration, the colour that metaphorically sees in the dark. Those choosing it are people with advanced perception – highly observant individuals, with clear sight, clear hearing, clear feeling. Indigo people in full health have powerfully focused intention and will easily create the circumstances that make them flourish.

A love for this colour indicates someone strong and dependable. Indigo people can rely on themselves, and can be relied upon. Other people tend to have great faith and confidence in this person, and rightly so: she can be wise and thoughtful as an advisor, and keeps her counsel, making her the safest confidant in the spectrum.

The indigo person is self-contained, and very much in control of his actions, his emotions and his destiny. Those on the indigo ray have the courage of their convictions, and tend to act upon them. They also have a fertile imagination which can be easily harnessed to any type of creative project, whether this be artistic, scientific or business. Indigo people take pride in their own culture and traditions, and also have a healthy respect for the thoughts and beliefs of others.

Indigo people have a strong mind and a powerful memory. They are able to co-ordinate many ideas or projects in their mind at any one time, thus they easily find themselves in positions of power and influence. Their clear, third eye quality makes them unusually perceptive, which allows them to see people and situations without illusion; these are not people to have the wool pulled easily over their eyes. While this is an obvious strength, it is a quality that can also cause the indigo person some pain: the truth is not always comfortable.

It is easy for indigo people to communicate with others from a place of authority and they are not phased by expressing what they believe to be right. This is a characteristic that gains them the respect of others; and also, on occasion, their hostility. The self-sufficiency that contributes to the indigo character can, if he lacks awareness, turn to or at least be perceived as arrogance and pride. Indigo is a colour associated with royalty, its power must be used with caution.

While the indigo person can be depended upon to keep the secrets of others, she may need to watch against a tendency to be unnecessarily secretive in her own life. This person is a shrewd observer, but there are times when she feels quite isolated, perhaps needing close company and being unable to find it. The dignity so natural to those on this ray can disguise a need in them sometimes to be supported as they support those around them; it is up to them to communicate this, if they wish to avoid having their strength taken for granted.

Indigo people have enormous powers of concentration and they are achievers. It is easy for them to invest great energy in a project; it is less easy for them to switch off the current and go home. They sometimes have need of the complementary energies of yellow, gold and amber to lighten up and let go of the responsibilities that so readily land on their shoulders.

# indigo flowers, oils and gems

INDIGO IS A fleeting colour which, apart from the evening sky, occurs only rarely in nature. Indigo flowers include irises, blue violets and pansies.

Frankincense, which is extracted from the resin of a tree, has the ability to slow down and deepen the breath, so its qualities are conducive to prayer and meditation. This has long been recognized within Christianity, where the gift of Frankincense was offered by one of the Magi to Jesus, and where its use has continued in the celebration of Mass. The delicious, uplifting smell can be obtained by burning the resin in a dish, and it is also available as an aromatic oil.

Lapis lazuli is a deep royal blue stone, interlaced with flecks of gold. It is associated with spiritual awakening, divinity and protection from depression. Sodalite, also deep blue, is a calming stone, which slows the activities of the body and induces sleep. It also encourages spiritual awareness and psychic perception.

# indigo health and healing

INDIGO INFLUENCES the head, especially the eyes, ears and nose, as well as the pituitary gland. This deep colour has the capacity to stimulate and strengthen the memory and also to relieve physical pain and induce relaxation and sleep.

When the indigo energy is out of balance, a person may suffer headaches, sleeplessness, anxiety or depression. The colour has been used in psychiatric care to pacify nervous disorders and neutralize obsessions and deep fears. It is also useful in treating sinus problems or infections of the upper respiratory tract. Indigo is helpful for tired eyes. While this colour is less prolific in nature than some, Frankincense oil, lapis lazuli and sodalite gemstones can be harnessed to potent effect. The petals of indigo flowers such as pansies have been used to relieve eye strain: placing them on closed eyelids for a few minutes will soothe discomfort and pain. There are also a number of foods, such as blackberries and figs, olives and seaweed, which bring in the indigo ray where it is needed.

The deep memory of indigo people is a strength and also a weakness that can affect their health. Letting go of painful memories is a challenge emphasized on this ray. Indigo is closely related to the intellect, and it is the intellect that has responsibility for monitoring the mind. An empowered, truly indigo person is one who claims authority by choosing only those thoughts that bring a positive outcome. Small amounts of indigo used in interiors, particularly when balanced with the complementary energies of yellow and gold, encourage this process, as do indigo clothes – or indigo used in visualization.

# INDIGO symbols

The **night** sky, studded with **stars**

**Deep** blue sea: **impenetrable**

**Third eye**: **all-seeing**

**Royal blue** robes: **royalty**, authority

**Navy blue**: armed forces, service, **loyalty**

# INDIGO symbols

**Sodalite** gems: opening new **perspectives**

**Frankincense**: spiritual **authority**, gift of kings

**Lapis lazuli** gems: **integrity**, spiritual awakening

**Royal blue ink**: deep-coloured but almost **transparent**

# indigo foods

INDIGO RELATES more to the mental than the physical faculties, and the effect of indigo foods is sedative and calming. They encourage peace of mind and are helpful in tranquillizing any kind of nervous disorder. Indigo promotes lucidity and understanding, so these foods also play a part in detoxification, particularly on a mental level. Late afternoon and early evening are ideal times to take in the indigo ray in your food, to help in winding down and to give the body the best opportunity for purification.

The colour contains a proportion of black, and many indigo foods are blackish in appearance. They strengthen the body when a person is suffering from respiratory tract infections, problems with the eyes, ears, sinuses or nose, or headaches and sleeplessness.

Indigo fruits: blackberries, blackcurrants, black cherries, fresh or dried figs, and currants. Indigo vegetables: mushrooms, black olives, black beans, soy sauce and miso, as well as certain seaweeds. Indigo spices: black pepper and juniper berries.

# indigo in love

THE INDIGO PERSON has a reflective, meditative nature. It is vital that an indigo partnership is based primarily upon mental and spiritual harmony. The love life of an indigo person, who is faithful and monogamous, will thrive as long as it is built on this firm foundation of spiritual congruency. Where this exists the intense, powerful indigo person is also very passionate. The sharply observant nature of an indigo person is reassuring to her partner, who feels secure in the knowledge that he is deeply recognized and appreciated.

Indigo people need periods of peace and solitude and apparent inactivity. It is important for the partner of an indigo person to understand and respect this need for personal space; and also to know that the indigo character is vulnerable to despondency and feelings of loneliness. Indigo people need to be understood as well as trusted; they must have space but they also thrive on warmth.

These highly responsible people can sometimes take life too seriously. Every partnership needs laughter and relaxation, playtime as well as work. The indigo partner may also slip into the driving seat a little too often for his mate's comfort: with his easy competence, he may forget that an intimate friendship needs equality and balance. The observant and thoughtful indigo qualities are quick to respond to disharmony and redress the balance.

# indigo parents

INDIGO PARENTS are wise, strong and authoritative, creating a stable structure for children. The vision that characterizes people on this ray enables them to keep an overview in the care of children. They are no more swayed by changing fashions in child rearing than in any other field and grasp easily what will best serve the highest good of each individual youngster. As parents they are thoughtful, caring and responsible. Their observant quality keeps them alert to their children's needs and they are often well tuned psychically to their feelings and thoughts.

An indigo person is a stimulating parent, as her own level of curiosity is high and quickly engages her whole attention on whatever interests her. She may lead by example and encourage a child towards his fullest efforts and potential. Because the indigo parent believes in his own power, he is able to raise children who are confident and self-reliant.

Indigo people have a perfectionist streak, expecting a lot from themselves. These people can be tough disciplinarians, which works only as long as it is balanced by affirmative messages of love. They may need to be careful not to put undue expectations on their children's performance; and they should guard against their own tendency towards all work and no play.

# indigo children

INDIGO CHILDREN often feel different from other people. They see beyond the illusions that keep others content and often have quite marked psychic abilities. These are generally interesting children to be around and also quite demanding mentally, being insatiably curious and asking endless questions. They sometimes have an uncanny – and disconcerting – way of being ahead of their teachers.

One of the striking features of indigo children is the force of their memory. They have a great capacity for absorbing and retaining information. Their mental powers are above average and this strong memory is a great asset in their schooling.

An indigo child is not only quick to learn but also highly imaginative. He or she loves to involve herself in subjects such as music and the dramatic arts. They easily find themselves in leadership positions, and it is frequently the indigo child who has the ideas that spark a creative project into action.

The child with a marked degree of indigo is often a loner. He may also suffer from loneliness. Indigo friendships are close and fairly intense rather than numerous, as these children rely primarily on their own resources.

# indigo in the home

INDIGO IS THE darkest hue, and can therefore have the effect of absorbing most of the light in a room if used in quantity. All deep blues have a strong impact. They are also restful if used in rooms where there is sufficient natural light. This intense, powerful colour is essentially sedative in its effect, so it is best used in rooms where you relax after mental work, or for meditation rooms, or for sleep. For those who need substantial exposure to this ray, it can be used in the bathroom to dramatic and exciting effect. If your physical energy is already low, however, the colour is best avoided in all but small quantities.

Indigo can be very well used as an accent colour on doors and skirting boards, or in curtains and soft furnishings. When placed in conjunction with its complementary colour, deep yellow, the effect is strong and uplifting. The yellow raises the spirits while the indigo deepens the breath. Diluted with white, the colour forms a very restful pale indigo – a cross between pale blue and lavender. This is a good colour for bedrooms, as it helps sleep and relaxation without being too sedating for a dynamic start in the morning.

This deep blue, the colour of royalty, brings a feeling of substance and solidity into any area of the home. Bring the colour in through ornaments and pictures, cushions and curtains, crockery and glass.

# indigo at work

THE INDIGO PERSON is the natural commander. The idealism of indigo combines with the ability to influence people to form a special combination of talents. People on this ray can handle large quantities of information. They have strong memories and an easy ability to prioritize, so their organizational skills are strong. With the indigo gift for clarity and deep sight, this person can also see the strengths and weaknesses of others.

Indigo talents can be well harnessed in all aspects of management. Like the conductor of an orchestra, the indigo person knows instinctively who fits in where, and when. In good balance, indigo people can equally apply such skills to themselves: their level of self-awareness and command fits them naturally for positions of responsibility and power.

Indigo people often choose work in which they can teach or influence people in a positive way. Always seeing beyond the surface to people's truth and their real needs, this person may be a counsellor, a spiritual teacher, an artist, a musician or music therapist, a writer of books or music. In business, she will hold a key position and be much relied upon. Or the psychic indigo edge might lead him towards clairvoyant or parapsychological work. Whatever indigo people do, they are more likely to lead than to follow.

# indigo visualization

Lie down, close your eyes and take some deep breaths. As you breathe, imagine that you are watching the sky as it moves from the clear blue of the daylight hours to the deep indigo of mystery and magic, and feel the indigo ray as it enters your body through your head, into your eyes and your ears. This is a colour of sudden revelation. You are flying, gliding through the indigo sky as day turns to night and the stars are switched on, one by one like little electric lights, decorating the sky. All around you is the colour indigo, touching your skin and wafting through your lungs and mind. It washes through you and around you, reminding you that your creative possibilities, like the ever-expanding universe, are infinite. This is the land of your dreams, where you can be all at once on earth and in heaven. Indigo is a catalyst: it offers swift, deep transformation to your perceptions and your thoughts. Allow the colour to melt away the blocks that have slowed your eyes and dulled your ears. Drink it deep so that you will awaken with renewed senses.

When you have received all that you need of this ray, take a few deep breaths and open your eyes.

# indigo clothes

THIS COLOUR CARRIES an air of sobriety and power along with a sense of loyalty and conscientious service. People who wear this colour frequently thrive on responsibility and decision-making. They are competent and intelligent. They derive peace from the order and structure that is essential to their performance.

Indigo is a good colour to wear when you wish to feel self-contained or when you need to inspire the confidence and trust of others. It also connects you to your higher mind functions, helping you move beyond illusion to the full truth of a situation. On the other hand, it exacerbates feelings of isolation or depression and points to an intolerance of commotion and a lack of spontaneity, humour or fun. Its complementary colours of yellow, amber and gold give indigo an immediate lift and can look stunning. Green also harmonizes gently with indigo to bring in relaxation and self-expression.

Indigo is flattering to those with yellow or red tones in their natural colouring, but for those who lack yellow it can have an ageing effect. Lapis lazuli jewellery, worn around the neck or ears, brings in a potent dose of indigo energy for those who need it but whose natural colouring lends itself better to the warmer rays.

# indigo in a nutshell

THE INSIGHT, the visionary nature and the powerful command of indigo are exceptional. Hold to your vision and others will follow. Avoid the temptations of standing too far apart from others: arrogance or over-coolness will cut you off and leave you isolated. Let your hair down and have fun. Your key strength in love, life and work is focussed intention. Stay peaceful, be true to your purpose and concentrate your vision. Bring more indigo into your life when you need to:

- Slow the breath and find a deep sense of calm, particularly during times of anxiety when you tend to hold on tight, or breathe too shallow and fast.

- Bring more power and effectiveness into your communications; feel the confidence and strength that other people sense you have and which you may not yet have felt able to access.

- See or understand more deeply some issue that is occupying your mind. Begin to understand the causes of depression and loneliness that may seem to have pursued you from time to time throughout your life. Ease headaches and sleeplessness.

- Get in touch with the masculine, authoritative aspect of yourself, no matter which sex you are, and your ability to know your own mind, so that you can take full control of your life.

- Bring your dreams to earth!

violet

Violet is the final colour in the seven principal rays comprising the full rainbow spectrum of light. The violet area of the spectrum covers shades from the near-indigo of irises to the redness of purple and magenta. This is the ray that balances the opposing energies of blue and red, containing the strength of each. The wavelength of pure violet is the most calming of all the colours. This very calmness is, in part, what gives this ray its powerful healing quality. Violet can soothe the pains of the body and pacify the turbulence of the mind, restoring order out of chaos. This colour represents the maturity and the calm that comes at the end of a cycle of activity. The violet ray acknowledges the learning of lessons and it also heralds deep change and transformation. This is a colour that brings to mind bishops as well as kings: spiritual wisdom and authority as well as temporal. It denotes the surrendering of personal desire in favour of a greater cause. There are cultures where it is believed that to sleep between violet sheets promotes longevity. Those who find themselves frequently drawn towards this ray are people who may have lived and endured much, and who have learned from their experience.

# violet people

VIOLET PEOPLE in good balance are natural healers and born pioneers and leaders, radiating peacefulness, a sense of authority and the energy for positive change. A preference for violet indicates someone of maturity as well as strength. Violet people have a deep well of inner resources. They also have a dedicated sense of service, and will willingly sacrifice their own personal desires if there is a greater cause at stake.

The violet person has spiritual stamina, which gives her great staying power. She is able to keep focused on her goal even through times of great change and upheaval. She may also be an idealist, and something of a perfectionist: whatever she turns her hand to will be done thoroughly and well. Violet points to a deep and independent thinker, with less need than many for outside approval of their point of view. The violet individual is immune to waves of fashion in behaviour or thought.

Violet has a natural ability to bring an atmosphere of calm reassurance to those in trouble, and to soothe their grief or pain. The violet person shoulders responsibility not only for himself but also for many of the other people in his life. This can make the burdens of this ray rather too heavy, particularly as such people are subject to despondency or real depression; and it also shelters others from their need to take responsibility for themselves.

The idealism that often accompanies those linked to violet can make it hard for them to live in the real world, when the world of their creative imagination may seem preferable. It can be easier for people of this vibration to link into the spiritual realms than to relate solidly to the here and now. This can result in a tendency towards escapism: the violet person sometimes perceives what she would like to see rather than what is. In order to overcome this, it is helpful for a violet person to focus on her body and particularly her feet. The use of red energy can also help. Foot massage, red socks, red shoes or bare feet: all these help the violet person to keep his feet on the ground.

Violet people can be perfectionists. This gives a controlling edge to the violet character, sometimes making them tough on themselves and others. It can be hard for this person to acknowledge that another person is able to do a job as well as they can.

Violet is about balance: hot and cold, masculine and feminine, logic and intuition. Where violet energy needs topping up, its absence may show up as something of the *wounded healer*: while violet people have often listened to the grief of others, it has perhaps been difficult to unburden themselves of their own difficulties and sorrows. For the same reason, in his unfailing sense of responsibility towards all that surrounds him, this person is often subject to deep fatigue, and he may sometimes lose sight of all the fun that others seem to enjoy.

It is important for those on this ray to bring in some of the balancing energy of yellow, amber and gold, to encourage them to let their hair down, look to their own wishes and needs, and give themselves an opportunity for enjoyment and relaxation.

# violet flowers, oils and gems

NATURE OFFERS a wide range of violet flowers, including violets and violas, pansies and lavender. Lavender has a cleansing as well as a soothing effect; violets are believed to help in connecting with loved ones who have died.

Essential oil of lavender has many uses; among others, it is antiseptic, tranquillizing, and soothing for physical pain. Lavender oil can also be used in the bath or sprinkled on the pillow to calm fevers and other over-active conditions, or applied directly to areas of pain. Waft it from a vaporizer and be prepared to find yourself dropping off to sleep. Violet oil also has antiseptic and healing properties and is particularly helpful in treating skin problems.

Amethyst is a protective and healing stone, which has the ability to restore the natural state of balance. It calms anger and passion, dispelling negativity in any form, and encourages spiritual awakening. Fluorite, which generally combines the colour turquoise with violet, lifts the energy towards universal, unconditional love. It also has a strengthening effect on the bones.

# violet health and healing

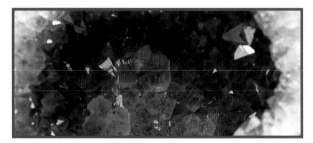

THE VIOLET RAY relates to the crown chakra. In very good balance it can represent the crowning glory of health, maturity and an equilibrium that will withstand almost any knocks. This condition is rare! The violet person, who so often takes on too much, can suffer exhaustion, listlessness and depression. The cheerful and complementary hues of yellow, amber and gold can be a better antidote for this condition than violet itself.

The strength of the violet ray is also its weakness: violet people live much in their heads. They are constant thinkers, full of ideas and thoughts that may fail to reach the body, resulting in headaches, pain in the neck and tiredness. Violet is often the best colour remedy here, bringing the body/mind balance that is lacking. Ingested in your food, worn around the upper part of the body, added to the bath, sprayed into the aura, or contemplated in meditation, violet will act to redress the balance that is lacking.

Violet can be used to calm tumours and relieve headaches and concussion. It balances the two sides of the brain so can also be used in treating epilepsy. For severe disorders of this kind, light therapy in treatments such as colourpuncture brings remarkable results. Ultra-violet is used in orthodox medicine for calming over-activity.

Above all, to maintain a state of health and happiness, it is essential for the violet person to find a balance between the need to give and the tendency to burn out.

# VIOLET symbols

**Bishops and cardinals**: **spiritual** authority

**Lent**: **mourning**

**Violet** sheets: **longevity**

*Shrinking violets*: **shyness**, remaining in the background

# VIOLET symbols

**Fluorite** stones: strength, **spirituality**

**Amethyst** gems: **purification**, elevation

**Purple fruits**: end of the **season**

*Purple* *passages*: **depth** of feeling and perception

# violet foods

VIOLET IS THE RAY that balances the active, dynamic and physical energy of red with the calming, uplifting and more spiritual energy of blue. It brings together the yang and the yin, the warm and the cool. Violet foods are ideal for those seeking equilibrium, and such a state of inner harmony promotes creativity as well as peace of mind. The violet area relates to the crown of the head, thinking, and the pineal gland. Violet calms headaches and helps in the treatment of tumours and concussion. Violet foods can therefore play a significant part in healing any mental disorders and imbalances in the nervous system. The effect of all violet foods is tranquillizing and soothing; they are particularly well suited for the later times of day, before the body settles down to rest.

Violet fruits: purple grapes and plums. Violet vegetables: purple cabbage, red onions, purple sprouting, globe artichokes and aubergines. Violet herbs: lavender, thyme and sage.

# violet in love

VIOLET PEOPLE do nothing by halves. Spiritually, emotionally and sexually, their relationships are intense. When the violet person commits himself to a partner or a friend, it goes deep and lasts long; and his natural tendency to care for and support others creates strong foundations. The violet mate is devoted, loyal and responsible, with a great capacity for the kind of inner balance that reflects itself in her outer experience.

The idealism of the violet character is strong but it may pose challenges at times: the violet tendency to see things as they believe they should be rather than as they are can prevent them from appreciating and enjoying what is already in their lives. The violet person's great plans and visions, too, may be all-consuming, making her demanding and controlling. Violet people sometimes have unrealistic expectations of those around them, so that a close partner may feel under pressure. It is important for violet people to be self-aware so that they keep their expectations and the atmosphere light.

People on the violet ray are generally soothing and nurturing to be around. If they are gentle on their partner and, equally important, on themselves, their love life will be warm, solid and fulfilling.

# violet parents

BEING A NATURAL healer, the violet parent soothes and calms all whom she touches. Violet parents are protective in the care of their children, while also ready to recognize the individuality of each one of them. They are responsible, taking an active, involved part in all aspects of their children's lives.

Violet people are the most dependable in the spectrum. This strength creates a strong foundation of security for children, who know that whatever happens, their parent will cope. Such parents are gentle and observant of those in their care and are keen to shield them, as far as is realistic, from the stresses of the adult world. While the violet adult may have something of a pre-disposition towards depression, in general she is stable and her moods are reliable.

The integrity, the staying power and the solid dependability of violet parents is a great gift for a child in their care, who derives a fundamental optimism and sense of strength, honesty and commitment to effort from the role model they provide.

The natural ebullience of children may sometimes be stressful for the violet parent, whose nature is quiet and peace-loving. The violet person's interests are often directed towards mental, adult occupations, so it is important for him to take necessary time out for himself, to ensure that he receives the personal nourishment he needs and to avoid the draining effects of over-preoccupation with child care.

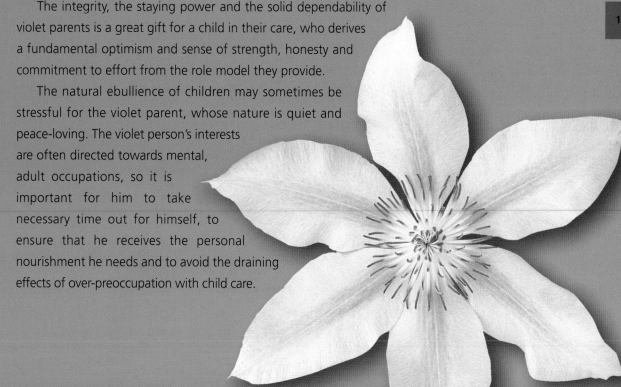

# violet children

VIOLET CHILDREN are sensitive and idealistic. They are dreamers, often creating rich worlds through their play and sometimes in their work. They have a good capacity to concentrate but only if a subject grips their attention. If they are bored, as they may be when asked to play certain sports, for example, or by some of the more practical demands of their education, they are liable to become distracted. The violet child may be chastised for lack of attention when in reality he has been involved in some other project, mental or otherwise, which felt more important at the time. This child does not set out to be disobedient or uncooperative and criticism goes deep.

The violet child often has a marked degree of independence, born of a strong mental capacity and wide personal resources, but she is also faithful and dependable. These children are rarely gregarious but they make firm friendships. Other children generally like and respect them and easily come to trust them as they know they can rely on their violet integrity for fair play and consistency. Violet children can seem old before their time, with a wisdom and a sense of responsibility beyond their years. It is helpful to balance the energy of a violet child with the use of warm, carefree rays from the orange and yellow range.

# violet in the home

VIOLET IS THE most steadying of all the rays. It balances the hot, stimulating energy of red with the cool, calming influence of blue. The deeper violet tones are rich and royal, while the paler tones of lavender and lilac are gentle and protective – and warmer than blue. The colour in any variation encourages the flowering of intuition and the deeper senses, so it is good for quiet rooms where you spend time in contemplation, meditation or study. This colour also promotes self-respect, strength and self-reliance. As this ray can be difficult for many people to wear, it may work better for some when brought into walls and furnishings.

The deeper tones need reasonably large spaces and good light, unless used only as an accent colour. Its cool, calm nature requires light even in the paler tints: as long as there is good natural light in a room, lavender or lilac provide a restful background colour, and the antiseptic, cleansing properties associated with the lavender plant combine well with white to make a space refreshing and relaxing.

Violet is a particularly helpful ray in times of change. This balanced colour promotes feelings of stability and security: it provides a background of peaceful protection for children and for teenagers as they go through the life-shifts of the adolescent years.

# violet at work

THE INDEPENDENCE of violet people, their capacity for deep understanding, their creativity, integrity and idealistic commitment to service are their hallmarks. Violet people do well when they bring these features together, finding a way to be creatively independent. Whether they will it or not, violet people radiate a soothing, healing quality which makes their presence invaluable in any workplace. As usefulness is a higher priority to the violet person than money or fame, it is not difficult for any violet individual to find work that is rewarding and fulfilling.

Violet people are pioneers: they have the dedication to push the frontiers of knowledge, often being those who expand the boundaries of science or the arts. These visionary qualities of violet also suit them well to media work, as long as the nature of the work feels worthwhile. The vision of these individuals may also be the driving force behind creative new developments in business; as long as they feel needed and worthwhile, they do not seek overt acknowledgement or fortune. Artists and leaders in any field resonate with violet. They welcome any situation in which they can contribute to positive change. The violet person could be a writer, teacher or designer; a doctor of many kinds or a nurse. They may be a politician or a rocket scientist, but work as a salesperson or an advertising manager is a less likely choice.

# violet clothes

VIOLET CLOTHES carry the soothing, reassuring effect of this ray but their appearance tends to suit only those with appropriate natural colouring. Those with red hair or a certain amount of yellow tone in their skin can be flattered by wearing this colour; those of olive complexion and jet black hair set off violet beautifully; those with complexions leaning more towards the blue end of the spectrum look washed out.

The violet ray promotes feelings of peacefulness and calm, it connects you with your intuition and gives you a deeper sense of yourself. It also has the effect of stimulating latent creativity, strengthening the sense of value in whatever you wish to communicate through any kind of creative endeavour. The violet ray reminds you of your strength, integrity and wholeness and it sends a message of quiet, peaceful authority to those around. Worn at work, it indicates a conscientious attitude. At home, it radiates a caring, healing quality.

If the colour does not work for you visually, amethyst and fluorite worn in jewellery will bring in the qualities of this ray.

# violet visualization

LIE DOWN and close your eyes. As you breathe in, take your attention to the crown of your head. See a violet light filling your crown and moving downwards through your body. This is the violet flame of transmutation, which burns up all negativity and petty concerns, helping you to focus on all that promotes your highest good. Feel the gentleness of the violet ray as it surrounds you. Be aware of the support offered by the universe. This is a ray of deep balance, maturity and completion.

Absorb the violet energy and accept its healing nourishment, which regenerates the body as it refreshes the mind. Feel the strength and courage, the balance and sense of fullness that permeate your cells as the violet ray penetrates your awareness more deeply. Take the violet light to areas of pain, allowing it to wash through them, bringing soothing balm, relieving distress.

When you feel you have absorbed all you need of this ray for the moment, encourage the movement of vital energy from your crown down to your feet. In your own time, open your eyes.

# violet in a nutshell

WITH YOUR WISE, supportive, reflective nature, you are a natural adult. Hold on to the soothing healing energy that others love, but before your back breaks, remember that you also need a measure of support. Focus on love and happiness to avoid the painful trap of harbouring grief. Your key strength in love, life and work is going with the flow of perpetual change. Change is the only constant, which turns problems into exciting opportunities. Use violet energy when you need to:

- Recover from an episode involving grief and/or loss of some sort: maybe a bereavement, a divorce, or a severe accident. Convalesce after illness, or calm over-active conditions of the body or the mind.

- Prepare for a major life change ahead, such as retirement or moving house, or recover from one that has already happened.

- Find a renewed feeling of faith, and connect with a true sense of purpose in your life, perhaps after a period of sadness, disillusionment or depression.

- Discover deeper personal resources and independence.

- Help a teenager through some of the physical and hormonal changes and other troubles associated with adolescence.

black

Black is what the eye sees when all colours are absorbed rather than reflected, so it is not a colour in the usual sense of the word. Black does not occur in nature: what may look black is invariably a deep shade of brown or indigo. Pure black has limited uses within colour therapy and psychology, but it is helpful when a person needs protection. The philosopher and colour theorist Rudolph Steiner saw colour as the borderline between black and white: it is what happens when light is shone into darkness. Understood in this way, black can be seen as a colour of mystery and potential. It is associated with silence and with the darkness of the night, when all is at rest. Black is also connected with a strong sense of discipline, order and self-control. It indicates the structure that underlies organization and which is ultimately very freeing. When someone is consistently drawn towards black, this may indicate a state of depression or despair. This person may suffer black moods and have little belief in themselves or in the future. In this case, black is the tunnel without the light at the end of it. Black stones are protective against the negative forces that encourage such a state of mind, ushering in a sense of grace and peace.

# black in the home

WHERE WHITE REFLECTS nearly 100 per cent of the light that falls on it, black absorbs something in excess of 60 per cent, and thus dramatically darkens a room if used in quantity. It can, however, be used to striking effect as an accent colour, in conjunction with whites and creams, where it can help to focus the concentration and heighten a person's efficiency. Grey can have a similar effect, but works better alongside pink or blue. While it can make an impressive office or reception area, black is best avoided within social areas or kitchens, except as a detail, as it has a depressing effect on the appetite and often on conversation.

Black flowers, such as roses and black violets, make an arresting display in any room, as well as in the garden.

# black clothes

THE FREQUENT choice of black clothes often indicates a person who is strong willed, but who likes to remain in charge of situations by keeping control of information. This colour is popular with artists, whose potential is kept in the dark until it is expressed through their paints. It is also much worn by teenagers, where the combination of protection and uniformity makes them feel safe as they move through adolescence. It is a very striking backdrop for gold jewellery and for bright colours. It also sets off colours such as pale blue and pale pink. It is always available within fashion worldwide; but because of its negative aspects, this colour is best kept for occasional use.

white

White is wide-reaching and panoramic. It is the source of full-spectrum light from which all other colours spring, reflecting all colours in equal measure. This is the blank page that contains all possibilities; the brilliance that fuels great minds and inventions; the spark that gives rise to life. White is a colour of choice: it may be the transparent joy of sunlight, or it may suggest the opaque mistiness of a cloud. This is the light that penetrates dark corners and has the capacity to wash away sorrow and sadness, making all things clean. It is purifying for the body and also for the mind. White reveals or it hides; it is everywhere and nowhere. It is a karmic colour that may represent the innocence, freshness and purity that speaks as it finds, or it may signify the whitewash that hides the truth. The white light may contain all colours, or none. The colour is reflective and protective: it may be a bright light, a mirror or a shield. This all-encompassing waveform may show the aspiration to reach for the stars, the courage to face the searchlight, or the emptiness that seeks colour anew. This is a colour of breadth and depth; the panorama that contains the whole picture, but may yet be undefined.

# white people

WHITE PEOPLE have the potential to be exceptionally broad-based and well-balanced. This is the light that contains all colours, so white people have wide abilities and plenty of choice. They are always individualists and frequently loners. People are often drawn towards white at times of change and growth, when new thoughts are forming and they are ready to discover who they are.

In good health and balance, the white person is confident, clear in his goals and optimistic. White can also represent uncertainty or the absence of self-knowledge. The white person sometimes likes to keep her options open so that she can be everywhere and nowhere, unlimited by firm commitments or decisions. People may also be drawn to white at times of confusion, doubt or grief. The wide potential contained within this colour is a gift but it may be hard for a white person to know who he is.

White is a colour of clarity and freshness. This person may be transparently open, honest and pure. Or, he may be a mirror, reflecting the truth back to others while himself remaining hidden. The clarity of white bestows clear sight: the white person generally sees more deeply than average: she knows that she is not easily deceived. She may suffer the hostility of others who, in her presence, see themselves too clearly for comfort. White people also have the capacity to look at situations from a fresh angle. The white take on things is often a stimulus to others to sit up and think anew.

White signifies cleanliness and simplicity. The white person travels light. He dislikes clutter, emotional or physical, so in good balance he faces things squarely, lives tidily and achieves great things through his clear focus and his endeavours to keep life simple.

# white health and healing

WHITE IS HELPFUL in achieving all-round balance, to produce optimum physical health. It supports the energetic body in achieving a balance of the aura and chakras. Clear quartz crystals will speed and empower this process.

The person frequently drawn towards the colour white is often someone of spiritual strength and vision; but it is not uncommon that they have encountered some difficult experience and feel physically depleted or washed out, as though all the colour has gone from their life. This is the time for them to notice the colours that draw them, and to use these to restore their strength. White sprays are an easy and deep-acting method of restoring overall balance (see Websites).

White people sometimes need the courage to confront the painful emotional issues they have brushed aside, if they are to access their potential and live life to the full. The failure to do this is what sometimes leads white people to suppress emotional pain, which eventually expresses itself in bodily imbalance. The clear nature of water makes this an element related to the colour white. Treatments such as colonic irrigation, which use water to cleanse the gut and – even more powerfully – the emotions, address the deepest of white issues and wash out pains that have been buried for years.

Full-spectrum white light is used in orthodox medicine as a treatment for cancer. Sunlight destroys bacteria and encourages the immune system: colds and coughs occur much less frequently in the presence of light. Its over-use stimulates the immune system too much, however, encouraging skin cancers.

# WHITE symbols

A new **white** sheet of paper: **infinite** possibilities

**Bridal** dresses: virginity, **purity**, freshness

Chinese **funerals**: passage to **Heaven**

**Water**: **cleansing**

**Air**: stimulating, **refreshing**

**Snow** and **ice**: refreshing, **pure** as the driven **snow**

**Sunshine**: clarity.

# WHITE symbols

Mirrors: **reflection**

**Diamonds**: purity, **innocence**, faithfulness, higher nature

**White** noise: **empty** words

**White** flowers: **love** and devotion

Clear **quartz** crystals: **cleanliness**, strength, shattering of stagnation

Clear **glass**: **transparency**

Herkimer **diamonds**: expansion, sparkle, joy, effervescence

# white in the home

WHITE REFLECTS most of the light that falls on it, so it brings light to dark spaces. It expands an area, offering freedom and openness and creating simplicity. This is the colour of infinite potential and it is also undefined. It allows you the space to expand and explore; it encourages inner as well as outer purification.

Although clean and fresh, white is also stark and sterile, easily making a room feel anonymous and cold. The coldness of pure white suppresses individual growth and expression. Off-whites and warm whites, with subtle overtones of pink, peach, yellow or green, are more welcoming and nourishing than pure white; these blend with any other colour to create a soft and warm overall effect. Brilliant white, like flowers in nature, is effective in small quantities against deeper or more defined colours.

# white clothes

WHITE RADIATES an aura of cleanliness and crispness. It is good to wear when you need to feel fresh, alert and open-minded. Because of its tendency to reflect the light, it helps you to keep cool – physically in hot weather, and also emotionally and mentally. This protective quality of white gives the wearer time and space. White often indicates the need for a period of reflection before taking decisions or action, or making a commitment. Wearing white helps you to find clarity so that you can comprehend a situation more clearly. It clears prejudices and brings difficult issues to the surface, gently and painlessly, so that they may be understood and released.

The over-use of white is stark and draining. Energetically, white clothes keep at bay the colour rays you need for optimum health, so its use should be measured and tempered with the warmth and vibrancy of deeper hues.

# postcript

SOME YEARS AGO I received a letter from a nun, whose religious order had recently relaxed the ruling about the clothes they should wear. After years of being confined to a black habit, she was enjoying exploring the colours she had long craved, and she noticed that along with this process came a new discovery of herself and the package of talents and gifts, quirks and foibles that made her authentic and unique. She was continuing her work as a nun in service to others, but she was deriving more joy and satisfaction from the work than she had ever done during the time when she had remained anonymous, surrounded by the darkness of a single hue.

The experience of this one woman can be seen as a cameo of what each of us can experience in a lifetime, and also of what mankind is able to learn as we move forward into a time when each individual is regaining his personal sovereignty. Colour is the fast route to self-knowledge and to the individual responsibility which is the only road to real freedom. Knowledge of colour is present and alive within the unconscious of every one of us. It is for us to recognize the light and enlightenment that it contains, and to use it.

As we learn the simple, universal language of colour and imbibe some of what it has to teach in our daily lives, we can avail ourselves of its benefits on a daily basis. In a world where we are surrounded by colour as never before, our understanding of light and its uses is growing apace. All over the world, light therapies are advancing, bringing self-understanding and overcoming disease. Now is the time when every individual can reclaim the authority to decide his destiny, and discover his fullest possible health.

I hope these pages have offered you insights into some of the colour possibilities most immediately accessible: through the understanding of the messages it contains.

# recommended reading and websites

Allanach, Jack, *Colour Me Healing,* Element.

Amber, Reuben, *Color Therapy*, Aurora Press.

Berger, Ruth, *The Secret is in the Rainbow,* Samuel Weiser.

Chiazzari, Suzy, *The Complete Book of Colour,* Element.

Cumming, Catherine, *Colour Healing Home*, Mitchell Beazley.

Davis, Patricia, *Aromatherapy an A–Z,* C W Daniel.

Gimbel, Theo, *Healing Colour*, 5th Edition, Gaia Books.

Gimbel, Theo, *Healing through Colour*, C W Daniel.

Graham, Helen, *Healing with Colour*, Gill & Macmillan.

Holbeche, Soozi, *The Power of Gems and Crystals*, Piatkus.

Merivale, Philippa, *Colour Talks!*, Laramar.

Naess, Inger, *Colour Energy*, Colour Energy Corporation, Norway.

Verner-Bonds, Lilian, *Colour Healing*, Anness Publishing.

Verner-Bonds, Lilian, *Healing with Colour*, Anness Publishing.

Walker, Avery, *The Power of Color*, Avery.

www.color4Power.com:
Philippa Merivale's website, where you can obtain a mini 'readout', showing some of your dominant characteristics based on your colour choices. A variety of services is offered, including on-line readings, information on seminars, a guest forum, and articles and books.

www.entheosessences.com
This shows the range of Entheos Essences, which are beautifully coloured waters, made in California from a range of flowers and herbs, and easily applicable as sprays. They are potentized, swift and deep acting.

www.phytobiophysics.co.uk
An organization founded by Dame Diana Mossop, who has spent years researching the healing power of plants with special emphasis on their colour. It provides a range of Flower Formulas, referred to as 'Complete Harmony'. Simple to understand, easy to take and highly effective.

www.colourenergy.com:
This offers essences for creating coloured bath water: a pleasurable way of bringing a concentrated dose of the colour you need straight into your aura, your thinking and your life.

www.internationalassociationofcolour.com
The comprehensive website of the International Association of Colour, based in Cambridge, UK, which brings together information concerning many different colour disciplines, individual practitioners, links to websites and much more.

www.publicolor.org
This is a non-profit organization which, since 1996, has set about the revival of inner city areas in need. Through the power of colour, this organization is helping people revitalize their community. A very interesting read.

www.awakeningimages.com
This site features the beautiful, vibrational art of Ellen Epstein. Ellen's love for the ocean, nature, colour and humanity is the major source of inspiration for this artwork as well as her commitment to personal growth.

# index

**190**

# acknowledgements

PHILIPPA MERIVALE would like to thank Soozi Holbeche for her enlightening work on crystals and gems, some brief parts of which have been used in the text.

IMAGES SUPPLIED by Digital Vision, Chrysalis Books, Isobel Gillan, Philippa Merivale, Photo Alto and Photo Disk.

# about the author

PHILIPPA MERIVALE is a natural healer, a Reiki Master and a massage therapist, with training in NLP and homoeopathic medicine. Since discovering the effects of colour as a psychological and balancing tool in the early 1990s, she has sought to make this enriching and therapeutic energy widely available. For 12 years she has worked in the Far East, the Americas, Europe and the UK as a counsellor, teacher, writer and broadcaster, bringing colour therapy as a system for self-awareness and empowerment to the attention of people from all walks of life. She is also the author of *Healing with Colour*, *Colour Talks!*, and the forthcoming *Over the Rainbow*. Philippa lives with her husband and children in Oxford, UK, and California, US.